Assaulting the Gates

Assaulting the Gates

Aiming All God's People
at the Mission Field

Paul D. Borden

Abingdon Press
Nashville

ASSAULTING THE GATES
AIMING ALL GOD'S PEOPLE AT THE MISSION FIELD

No part of this work may be reproduced or transmitted in any form or by any means, electronic or mechanical, including photocopying and recording, or by any information storage or retrieval system, except as may be expressly permitted by the 1976 Copyright Act, the 1998 Digital Millennium Copyright Act, or in writing from the publisher. Requests for permission should be addressed to Abingdon Press, 201 Eighth Avenue South, P.O. Box 801, Nashville, TN 37202-0801 or permissions@abingdonpress.com.

This book is printed on acid-free paper.

Library of Congress Cataloging-in-Publication Data
Borden, Paul D.
    Assaulting the gates : aiming all God's people at the mission field / Paul D. Borden.
        p. cm.
    ISBN 978-1-4267-0220-4 (binding: pbk./trade pbk. adhesive-perfect : alk. paper)   1. Church growth.   I. Title.
    BV652.25.B67 2009
    269'.2—dc22
                                                                            2009026056

All scripture quotations, unless noted otherwise, are taken from the New Revised Standard Version of the Bible, copyright 1989, Division of Christian Education of the National Council of the Churches of Christ in the United States of America. Used by permission. All rights reserved.

Scripture quotations marked (NIV) were taken from the NEW INTERNATIONAL VERSION®. Copyright © 1973, 1978, 1984 by International Bible Society. All rights reserved throughout the world. Used by permission of International Bible Society.

09 10 11 12 13 14 15 16 17 18—10 9 8 7 6 5 4 3 2 1
MANUFACTURED IN THE UNITED STATES OF AMERICA

There are several individuals and groups to whom I want to dedicate this book:

The Numerous Effective Pastors and Church Planters in GHC

You are courageous women and men who model a missional commitment to Jesus Christ and to the church of Jesus Christ. You are the frontline soldiers God is using to transform communities and regions. You can stand proudly with the heroes of faith found in Hebrews, chapter 11.

Risk-taking Judicatory and Associational Church Leaders

You are the real heroes in denominational life. Many in your denominations probably do not know you or even know what you do. However, some of you are risking your positions, and in some cases your careers, to bring hope and salvation to people by seeing congregations transform from death to life. You are using your influence for the Kingdom rather than to maintain and build your denominational kingdoms.

Addison

You bring your parents delight. You give Jackson exercise. You make your grandparents so happy.

Teresa

You are my love, my friend, my companion, my mentor, my muse, and my joy. Without you I would be far less and our pastors and their families would be much poorer. Despite the sufferings of this life, you still live with zest and a deep desire to serve others well. Your care for those who have hurt you models the love of Jesus Christ. You are a hero of the faith!

Contents

Foreword

By Ed Stetzer

Change. It's what most churches need. But it's the one thing most churches aren't willing to do when it comes time to actually make changes. Many churches and their leaders get off track when trying to chart the course from plateau and decline to health and growth. Not knowing where to start, what to change, and how to get from one place to the other all contribute to their uncertainty.

Moreover, change involves what is unknown and uncomfortable for pastoral leaders and their congregations. In his book Assaulting the Gates, Paul Borden has charted a course for churches, their leaders, and denominational or network leaders to utilize so that the change process can be less intimidating.

But don't get me wrong—the process of change will still be painful. That's right . . . painful! If denominations, networks, pastors, and churches want to experience revitalizing change, some level of suffering will always be involved. Why does making these kinds of changes have to involve suffering? I'm glad you asked. Because not every person or church is going to want to change.

In reality, that's part of the curse of sin. We, and our churches and society and everyone in society, will always drift away from God and his plan for our lives and churches. Personal and congregational change usually means changing from the inside out. Sinful human nature rebels against that. After all, we know where to go and what to do. It's like the guy you hear about (of course, I've never done anything like this) who has been lost for an hour. His wife suggests stopping and asking for directions, but he knows that he's almost got it figured out. He *knows* exactly where he's going. Yeah, right!

Having said that, let's ask a few key questions for those courageous souls who want to chart the course and set sail for a new land. While it will involve some pain and suffering, the only way to experience the thrill of discovering a new land is to chart a new course, set sail for a new land, endure the hardships, and see what it's like on the other side. Where does the process of change start? What does the island of anemic, unhealthy, and diseased congregational life look like? What does the new land of health, growth, and reproduction look like? What does it take to get from one to the other?

Where to Start?

Only someone who has been stranded on a deserted island for the last thirty years could be unaware of the overall state of the North American church. Basically, things aren't looking too good. The statistics have been telling the listless story for quite a few years. But, as God always has a remnant, he raises up leaders and groups of people to chart a different course—to walk a different path so that his mission can be accomplished.

The place to start is to define reality. It's one thing to conclude that things are bad, but am I willing to admit that fact? I believe that many pastors, churches, and lay leaders know that things are not going so good, but many of them are not willing to take a stand and say some things need to change—I need to change, the church needs to change, and I am going to do whatever it takes to make some changes.

Stepping out of denial is a classic and foundational need. If you talk to people who have walked the path of recovering from addiction to alcohol or drugs or whatever, they will describe how important this is. It's not just recognizing that things are bad; it's having the guts to admit it and start getting some help. I love their line—"Your best thinking got you where you are." We have a lot of churches, pastors, and other leaders who need to start admitting that their best thinking got them where they are. And where are they?

What Does the Island of Misfit Churches Look Like?

In one of the "Rudolph, the Red-Nosed Reindeer" Christmas animations, the story turns to the Island of Misfit Toys. This is where all the reject toys end up because they are defective and kids don't want them. These toys don't fit in because they are put together with the wrong pieces, have the wrong color schemes, or make the wrong sounds. It's a sad place, but the toys just have a desire to be loved by some little boy or girl.

Unfortunately, a lot of our churches are like those misfit toys. Many of them have a desire to love and be loved by their communities, but they are not sure how to relate to their communities. Or, they have tried to relate in the wrong ways. Or, they aren't sure it's OK to relate to the communities at all; that might lead to compromise. And the people in the community look at many churches like those misfit toys: they don't have the right pieces, they appear outdated, or they speak another cultural language.

What else characterizes the deserted islands of anemic, unhealthy, and diseased congregational life? Most of it can be summarized by talking about church attitudes. Churches have attitudes? Yep! That involves how the people who make up churches think about their congregation, which then influences how they relate to the people and the community that surrounds them. Here are a few examples:

- The "sweet fellowship" church. This group of people convinces themselves that what matters is feeling good about being together. Translation: We wouldn't want too many, if any, new people coming in to mess up our wonderful time of being together.

- The "just spinning our wheels" church. This church may even be larger, but it functions and acts more like a machine. It may have lots of neat programs and ministries, but it's not really reaching the lost or making many new disciples. It's just going through the motions.

- The "retro" church. This is the church that hasn't figured out that they are living in another time zone. Basically, they are still doing things like they did "back in the day," which could mean doing church like it's 20, 30, or even 50 years ago. Whether they realize it or not, their church has become more like a bomb shelter than a combat force that God can use to win the war for lost humanity.

What Does the Land of Proliferating Churches Look Like?

Proliferate—to reproduce new parts in quick succession. That's ultimately the goal of *Assaulting the Gates*—the reproduction of new disciples and congregations. In reality, it's hard to imagine such a place because it's not actually happening much in North America. Therefore, maybe the best way to think about it is to think in terms of a family with a lot of kids.

When a couple sees having children as an expression of love and as a blessing from God, the adventure can be quite exciting. I have some friends, two different couples, who have managed to proliferate by having eight and nine kids, respectively. That's pretty much reproducing new "parts" in quick succession. Does all of that lead to some stress and chaos? Absolutely. Does that also (spring from and) lead to some fun and excitement? Most of the time.

Many people wonder how families of that size do it; that is, how they manage that many children. But with teamwork and sacrifice they make it work. It also requires the simple desire and willingness to receive new "parts." Think about the blessing those families receive and experience as they discover and enjoy the uniqueness of each child and watch how God uses each one.

Proliferating disciples and churches requires the same kind of dynamics—desire, teamwork, and sacrifice. In addition, the proliferation process will always involve some stress, tension, and chaos. But it will also lead to a whole lot of fun, excitement, and adventure. It allows churches and leaders to look back in the years to come and say, "Look at all the wild, crazy, and wonderful stuff that God did because we were willing to leave the island of misfit churches in order to find a new land."

How Do You Get There?

Well, that's why Paul Borden wrote this book. He's the one who can best answer that question. He has laid out a layered strategy and process that involves intentional learning clusters for pastors, congregational consultations with qualified coaches, missional covenants and action plans, and accountable models of leadership.

But, let me say this. This whole process must be rooted in prayer and renewed belief in Jesus. Remember how John described Jesus, the leader of the church, in chapter 1 of Revelation. May we be willing to serve him faithfully as he changes us and leads us to make changes:

Grace and peace to you from him who is, and who was, and who is to come, and from the seven spirits before his throne, and from Jesus Christ, who is the faithful witness, the firstborn from the dead, and the ruler of the kings of the earth.

To him who loves us and has freed us from our sins by his blood, and has made us to be a kingdom and priests to serve his God and Father— to him be glory and power for ever and ever! Amen. (vv. 4b-6, NIV)

I turned around to see the voice that was speaking to me. And when I turned I saw seven golden lampstands, and among the lampstands [representing his churches] was someone "like a son of man," dressed in a robe reaching down to his feet and with a golden sash around his chest. His head and hair were white like wool, as white as snow, and his eyes were like blazing fire. His feet were like bronze glowing in a furnace, and his voice was like the sound of rushing waters. In his right hand he held seven stars, and out of his mouth came a sharp double-edged sword. His face was like the sun shining in all its brilliance.

When I saw him, I fell at his feet as though dead. Then he placed his right hand on me and said: "Do not be afraid. I am the First and the Last. I am the Living One; I was dead, and behold I am alive for ever and ever!" (vv. 12-18a, NIV)

In the movie *Amazing Grace,* William Wilberforce faces the challenge of bringing systematic change to Great Britain. The opening lines of the movie tell of how Great Britain, the most powerful nation in the world at that time, had built its empire on the backs of slaves. Few considered anything wrong with slavery, and fewer still had the bravery to speak out against it. The film illustrates how difficult it can be to bring about systematic change, the kind of change that churches often need.

In the movie Wilberforce has struggled for years to abolish the slave trade, and finds himself worn out and discouraged. At that point, he meets his future wife, Barbara Spooner, who reminds him that swallowing back the bad taste in one's mouth is no way to get rid of it; the thing to do is spit it out. That's what many churches and their leaders need to do regarding plateau and decline: find a way to spit that taste out of their mouths. This book will help them do that if they are willing to face the challenge.

Paul Borden has outlined a system, a strategy, a process that will help surround churches and their leaders with the right kind of people and resources to get the job of revitalization done—and not just revitalization, but also reproduction and multiplication. I wholeheartedly agree with his insights about the ultimate goal of this process: the reproduction of new disciples and churches. If we are going to reach the lost of North America, revitalization must lead to multiplying reproduction.

Today, God has a remnant within the North American church. Paul Borden and the GHC (Growing Healthy Churches) Network is part of that remnant. They are helping lead some denominations, networks, churches, and pastoral leaders to chart a different course—to build bridges of change, revitalization, and reproduction from the remote, isolated islands of anemic, unhealthy, and diseased congregational life to the new, thriving, tropical lands of health, growth, and reproduction.

May the one who is alive forevermore give us new life in a new land!

CHAPTER ONE
A Valid Role for Dinosaurs

Introduction

Anyone alert to what is happening to the church of Jesus Christ in the continents most touched by the Protestant Reformation recognizes that it, the church, is losing the battle with the Evil One for the souls of people. Accompanying that loss is the ability to influence communities and nations for the kingdom of God. We have all heard the statistics about congregations on a plateau, in decline, or dying. Almost all denominations and associations of congregations recognize they are losing both dollars and influence, since the essence of all denominations, the congregations, are passing away. The overall picture is not bright. This situation is so different from what God is doing in the church south of the equator and in Asia. When one compares the former Christian world with the new emerging one, the decline of the former is staggering.

This is not to say there are not bright spots in the U.S., as is true in other industrial nations. There are many effective large congregations reflecting various philosophies of ministries, reaching multiple generations, using a myriad of strategies to make many more disciples for Jesus Christ. The planting of new congregations by risk-taking heroes of faith who are not only thinking outside the box but also looking way beyond any boxes is awesome to see. New paradigms and their reflected strategies for reaching lost people are being implemented in the conduct of missions both at home and overseas. When one sits with those involved in these arenas, one sees there is hope that God may yet again move in a mighty way.

There is one other strong ray of hope: what is happening within some denominations and congregational associations, not at the national level with rare exceptions, but at the local level. Groups of congregations, whether in regions, states, districts, conferences, associations, or the like, are beginning to act in intentional ways to transform older, dying congregations and start many new, vibrant ones. For example, our region, now called Growing Healthy Churches (formerly the American Baptist Churches of the West), has seen God do a miracle in the past decade. Not only has our God enabled us to see over half of our older congregations turn around and produce an abundance of new growth, God has allowed us to now plant more than seventy new congregations. The crucial statistic for us is baptisms (new disciples). Over a decade ago there were only eight hundred or fewer baptisms a year. Now there are more than four thousand baptisms every twelve months.

It is encouraging to see other groups of congregations take major risks in order to introduce change. As a result God is producing pastors, lay leaders, and congregations who are working effectively in making new disciples for Jesus Christ. This is happening in mainline circles, denominations that are not mainline, and associations of congregations that have often been known more for their independence and theological dogma than for evangelism and outreach. The Hit the Bullseye Network (HTBinc.org) now exists to provide a place for peer learning and resources for those leading these new, exciting changes.

However, when you put all of these great things together with all the success that God is producing through effective leaders and congregations, we are still losing ground nationally. While the younger generations are more and more spiritual in their approach to life, they are not finding meaning and fulfillment in Jesus Christ because the church overall is so weak, irrelevant, and devoid of life.

The Decline

In the history of the church of Jesus Christ no nation has possessed the resources to produce strong congregations like the United States of America. There has never been such a plethora of written and now digital media designed to help congregations succeed, Christians grow and minister with effectiveness, and disciples mature and reproduce. The making of books not only knows no end in the U.S., but the creating of seminars and training events seems almost infinite. No nation in the two thousand-plus years of church history has had more people and dollars available to see the

Great Commission successfully implemented. Yet not only is the church of Jesus Christ in this country in free fall as measured in market share; the entire nation is becoming increasingly pagan. The church of Jesus Christ in America has become a paper giant.

Obviously, there are many reasons for the current problems faced by the church. Theologians, historians, and sociologists with far more intelligence and expertise than this writer will be able to dissect the fall of the church. I also recognize that God may not yet be done with the church in our nation and we may still see another great revival. If our God allows the current trend to continue, however, the church will grow even more impotent and cease to influence our nation to pursue Godliness and holiness. I would like to share with you my perspective on why the current situation is a bleak one, despite pockets of spiritual vigor.

From its birth the church, which was designed to penetrate and change the culture, has been susceptible to being kidnapped by the culture. The Apostle Paul warned the Corinthian Christians to not capitulate to the philosophies and teachings of their culture. The early church was constantly struggling against being taken captive by those who wanted it to depart from the essence of the gospel. The Lord of the church appeared to the Apostle John and dictated seven letters to seven separate congregations, warning them that their candles would be snuffed out if they gave in to their respective local cultural issues. The church of Jesus Christ in the United States has not been immune to the siren calls of its culture.

Consumerism

If I were requested to find just one word that would describe our culture, the word would be *consumerism*. The economic teachings of capitalism, which have done so much to produce such a strong nation, have at the same time contributed to the decline of the church. The result is a church filled with people who are proud to be identified with Jesus Christ, yet who in their behaviors are far more concerned with having their needs and those of their families met than reaching those who are spiritually lost and separated from God. The amazing transformation in the congregations of our region has led to the production of numerous books, seminars (yes, we have contributed to the media glut), and trainings with denominations. Time after time I and many others have taught that the turn-around in the congregations of our region only happened as we began to focus more on others than on ourselves. Every time I teach this truth, I hear, "But what about us? What about our needs? What are you doing to help the Christians?" I have come to learn that we American Christians will reflexively make sure our needs are met, because after all, at our very core we are all consumers.

Consumerism in our congregations knows no generational differences. The only age differences are what the respective generations demand congregations to be and do in order to fulfill their consumer requirements. Often, older Christians are more concerned about their music and the issues of congregational structure that allow them to keep control of all that is happening. The baby boomers also want to maintain the forms of worship, the buildings, and the ministries they created in order to feel comfortable in their settings. The emerging generations want their expectations for size, groups, and media to be met in order for them to be happy. In most congregations, regardless of size, age, or backgrounds, it is all about "me" and my needs.

As I now work with a wide variety of denominations, I get to see how each has its own consumer demons that plague and thwart any ability to be missional. Usually it is a matter of insisting that certain ministries, once effective but now no longer so, continue in order to meet Christian consumer expectations. In some denominations it is using the church of Jesus Christ to run school systems that are rarely used to lead students to become disciples of Jesus Chrst. In other denominations it is maintaining institutions (schools, hospitals, nursing homes) that do good things, yet are killing the congregations who try to keep them going. This is particularly galling (at least to me) when often the children and adults being served could be cared for just as well in other ways, but Christian consumers can save money by having their denomination pay for it at the expense of mission. All denominations support ecclesiastical structures that continue to satisfy our denominational pride, yet put congregations under such financial bondage that they cannot engage in mission, even if they want to do so. Again, almost all denominations do this with camps that subsidize the attendance of children, most of whose parents could afford to pay more. At the heart of all of these endeavors is often a consumer demand that uses the church for that which the church was not intended to be used. We have created denominational money-changers who service consumer Christians at the expense of mission. The extreme left- and right-wing teachings of Christianity are less devastating to the church of Jesus Christ than the middle-of-the-road beliefs coming from the God of mammon.

Pacification

This consumer mindset has created another phenomenon that has it roots in the fuzziness of modern theology, while playing into the hands of the consumer Christ-followers. That phenomenon is the *pacification* of the church. I understand that this peaceful and pastoral mindset has come about in part as a reaction to rampant theological, sociological, and emotional fundamentalism that all denominations have had to face. Often the church of Jesus Christ was known more for what it was against, who it refused to tolerate, and how much it fought. Obviously such sectarianism is wrong. The reaction was also accompanied by modern theological thought that created fuzzy lines over those areas of orthodoxy that were becoming politically incorrect despite the teachings of Jesus Christ and the writers of Scripture. In fact, one way to create peace was to remove all dogmatism so there would be harmony.

These issues, coupled with those teachings of Jesus in relation to peace and harmony along with the command for unity, particularly in his body, have contributed to the view of the church as a place where strife and friction are absent. In one major sense that is true; God does not call us to fight with one another but rather to love one another as Christ loved the church. However, in congregations, denominations, and associations of congregations peace has been elevated in God's hierarchy of virtues. The church as an institution designed to meet consumer needs will not tolerate dissent, even if that dissent is to point out that the church has lost its way in relation to mission. Denominations all across the nation are losing people, dollars, and influence because they insist on peace at any price. Passive-aggressive behaviors (which include the creation of study groups, committees, and task forces as tools to avoid dealing head-on with substantive issues) have replaced confrontation. If we debate, we debate about structure—not theological essentials, not sinful behaviors, and definitely not heresy covered in politically correct language that redefines righteous standards and sinful actions.

In this process of pacification we have lost the idea that the church of Jesus Christ is to be militant against sin, the forces of evil, and unrighteous systems; we have forgotten that the church is called to convert those who use such systems to create injustice, war, and the great inequities of civilization. We have lost the idea of being soldiers of the cross, an army marching for the salvation of people, and lifeboat captains rescuing the perishing. Consumer Christians wanting to avoid the extremes of the Christian right and left desire a wonderful place to worship each Sunday that meets the needs of "myself and my family" without upsetting the "temporary Camelot" they call their congregations. Also, in most plateaued or dying churches the "silent majority" would rather allow the spiritual terrorist church bosses to keep the congregation from mission than raise issues that might upset the church's illusory peace.

I realize that a multitude of Christians might never read this book because they cannot get past the title, *Assaulting the Gates*. Such a term is too militant, as was *Hit the Bullseye* and *Direct Hit*. However, it is not important that such people read this book, since they are convinced that peace is a higher value in God's church than mission. Rather this book is for those who are frustrated with dying congregations, those who believe that Jesus has called us to mission and are willing to act. If you are one of these people, this book will both offer you hope and show you how to act on that hope. Jesus Christ is alive and well and is acting against the forces of evil. He is able and more than willing to bless those who will act in order to produce pockets of spiritual resurgence in the lives of congregations, denominations, and associations of congregations.

Role Clarification

Even as a highly inept handyman I know that hammers are great for pounding nails and horrible for turning screws. The right tool makes all the difference. The same is true for the various roles God calls us to fulfill. Pastors are called to "lead" sheep on a mission to attack the forces of evil. God calls upon sheep to attack roaring lions and expects them with his help to win far more often than they lose. Caregivers are those people God has called and gifted to employ mercy, compassion, tenderness, and other attributes to help those who are hurting and desperately need the help caregivers can provide. Let me employ a current metaphor. Pastors are like hospital administrators who raise funds, lead boards, fight with zoning authorities, deal with negative public relations issues, fight with insurance carriers and pharmaceutical companies, and cast vision for large medical facilities that serve communities well. Caregivers are like the doctors, nurses, orderlies, and other staff who attend to and care for patients. Both administrators and doctors and their support people care for the health of individuals and the communities they serve. Both roles produce service for the common good, yet wise corporate hospital boards are careful not to mix the two.

The church of Jesus Christ is declining in our and similar nations because, unlike hospitals, we have confused the role of pastor and caregiver. Denominations, seminaries, and congregations (we are all guilty) have allowed the caregivers to fulfill the role of pastor in most congregations. These caregivers are now also in positions of leadership in most denominations. In this process we have marginalized the pastors (those who lead because of their gifts or because God has called them to exercise such behavior). I continue to find that, in most denominational and associational groups I work with, the pastors of large congregations are at best left out of key positions, and at worst are treated as pariahs. Many see the larger congregations as unspiritual, even though they often produce more numerical and spiritual growth than the small congregations that constantly run off new people. We lift up the stories of how a faithful caregiver has helped one person because of an unending commitment of time and energy as the epitome of faithful service, while running down those who have created effective systems to reach many people with help during the same amount of time. The constant message seems to be that the smaller the congregation, the more spiritual the pastor must be.

One major result of such thinking is that those outside the body see the church as run by wimps. While this is true in one sense, it is not true in another. As one who has on several occasions been ministered to well by caregivers, I know that people with such gifts are courageous people. To hang in there long-term with hurting people takes a courage that only people with these gifts possess. Focusing always on the value of one at the expense of the many, however, ignores the role the Lord of the church had in mind for the body. Jesus had the ability to focus on both individuals and larger groups and calls the church to do the same. This means that the position of pastor must be for those who are willing to lead. As part of their leading, these pastors need to establish systems where caregivers can exercise their gifts and talents in ways that benefit the most people in need of their care.

Therefore, when you consider a consumer church that has been pacified and led by caregivers, the perception of wimpishness seems correct. The issue, though, should not be that one gift is better than another; it is that people are in positions that do not match the gifts God gave them, or they face condemnation when they properly use their gifts to focus on mission rather than caregiving. It is like asking a hammer to turn a screw or a doctor to administer a hospital. If this analysis is correct, it means that caregivers need to remove themselves from leading congregations that are serious about implementing the Great Commission. It also means that denominations, seminaries, and congregations need to become serious about recruiting, training, and recommending or placing those who lead over those who provide care. All Christians need to work out of both their gifts and their passions. Those with a passion and a gift for care need to be in places where they can best use that passion and gift. The same needs to be true for pastors. Our congregations and groups of congregations need to be led by those who possess a passion and a willingness to behave and act like leaders.

There are a multitude of theological and sociological reasons for the decline of congregations, denominations, and associations of congregations in this nation. However, the three I have described are major ones that often are not addressed in the life of the church. Failure to face these problems head-on will cause the decline to continue and even accelerate.

Valuable Dinosaurs

The majority of congregations in our nation belong to a group of some kind. That group is usually identified as either a denomination or an association. It is true that some congregations are independent of any group, or are a part of groups that prize and promote independence, but that is not the case for the majority. Both the denominations and associations of congregations, however, are akin to the dinosaurs—they are becoming more and more irrelevant and are in the process of becoming extinct, at least in their current form. The biggest reason lies in the drop of the number of congregants, producing fewer dollars to support the ministries and activities of these dinosaur organizations.

Let me say at this point that denominational leaders keep telling me that the changes they are now considering are because of the need for renewed mission. In part that is true. But if mission were such a high value, the tough decisions that keep being postponed until the dollars dry up would have been decided and implemented years ago. The groups of congregations most resistant to change are the ones that still have dollars or assets they can use, even if such usage cannibalizes their future ability to conduct ministry. The majority of excuses I hear for not making change and getting serious about mission (by those who claim that mission is the most important thing) are as unacceptable now as they were when the judges at the post–World War II Nuremburg trials rejected the same excuses. One prime example, "I would have liked to make the changes, but those above me just would not allow me to do so." I often wonder if such excuses will be accepted by our ultimate judge when the final judgment of the righteous and unrighteous is conducted.

There is hope for these dinosaurs, though. The hope is not to resurrect them to act as they did in their heyday. The hope is to leverage their vast influence (which they still have with the faithful) and the considerable resources (which are still available, though dwindling) in a new paradigm to produce transformation (and eventual reproduction) in their almost dead congregations. Also the hope is not to start at the top and produce change. Such a task will not work in most cases. People who have made it to any national position have too much at stake personally and institutionally to lead change. (There are rare exceptions, but in those cases it is because the group of congregations is relatively smaller and the leader is at a stage in life where a future with the denomination is no longer of major importance to her or him.) Rather the change must come from the congregations and that next tier of leadership that has the most influence with almost all congregations. In mainline circles that tier is called the middle judicatory. In other arenas it is the regional, state, district (or the like) denominational or associational people.

There is evidence to support having such hope. The miracle that God has performed and continues to perform in our region, Growing Healthy Churches, is one piece of that evidence. We constantly hear that older, established congregations cannot be transformed. In our region we know that is not the truth. Furthermore, there is a growing body of evidence that our region is not a one-hit wonder. God is beginning to work in such diverse groups as the Missouri Synod Lutherans, Church of God (Anderson), The United Methodist Church, The United Brethren in Christ, the Salvation Army, Seventh Day Adventists, Southern Baptists, and others who are now seeing some significant and sustained transformation in congregations. Most of these transformations are taking place in states, regions, and districts where the middle judicatory and local congregations are coming together to join God in God's mission for the church of making a continually growing number of disciples.

Denominations have many assets, and these assets need to be aligned to foster transformation and reproduction, not serve the denominational interests that currently take precedence over mission. First, they have the congregations, which means people, energy, time, dollars, and physical assets. Second, there is usually a strong sense of loyalty to the denomination by people who want to see mission occur under the auspices of the denomination. They have an infrastructure in place that, if used well, can serve the development of a strategy that leads to congregational transformation and then on to congregational reproduction.

The best assets for change in any denomination are those relatively few effective pastors, the ones whose congregations are increasing through evangelism growth. Unfortunately these pastors often live at the outer edge of denominational life because (1) they have been marginalized by the plethora of caregiver pastors leading declining congregations or (2) denominational personnel fear such leaders because they are often mavericks who do not need help from the denomination. Yet, if mobilized, these pastors have the experience, resources, and wisdom to lead local judicatories to revitalization as congregations are transformed.

We might view groups of congregations as sleeping giants waiting to either die or be shocked back into new life. Unlike the real dinosaurs, which are extinct, these organizational dinosaurs still possess enough life to be offered hope. Hope will not come in continual meetings focused on restructuring (rearranging the proverbial deck chairs on the Titanic) or in lifting up social and cultural issues as the touchstone of denominational vitality (tilting at windmills). Hope will come as congregation after congregation gets back to joining the Lord of the church in the mission the church was created to fulfill: making more disciples for Jesus Christ. Denominations and congregations may believe in various causes and act in a variety of ways to address social and cultural injustices. These beliefs and actions must always be subordinated, however, to the fulfillment of the mission; they must become part of the way that the mission is implemented.

If there is hope for our nation, and others like ours, it will be realized as the whole body of Christ becomes involved in fulfilling its role in accomplishing our Lord's mission for the church. The megachurches with all their associations, networks, conferences, and publications must do their part. The parachurch entities must do their part to promote mission and not pander to the social, consumerist, and political wants and desires of consumer-driven Christians. The mission agencies must help congregations connect mission here in our nation with mission elsewhere in the world. The educational entities must get back to developing students who graduate with a mission mindset. And the denominations and associations of congregations must use their last gasps of breath to risk striving for new life, rather than hoping to somehow survive while refusing to move from the 1950s to the twenty-first century.

Assaulting the Gates is written to only the last piece of this puzzle, denominations and associations of congregations. However, if this piece of the puzzle could fall into place, and the megachurches and other groups fulfill their roles, we would see again the church of Jesus Christ act like a mighty army going off to war, and for the first time in a long time in our spiritual experience it would be the right war.

A Strategy of Hope

The Theology and Theory

In talking about discipleship, Jesus observed that wise kings always count the cost of battle before engaging an enemy. Generals and commanders still act in accordance with such wisdom. Before any assault is started one thinks through what will be required to win the engagement. History is filled with the stories of unwise leaders who failed to take into account the cost of assaults, and who, as a result, lost battles and wars. The same principle is true in spiritual warfare. If our Lord created the church and promised it would grow in order to overcome the Evil One and his minions, then leading congregations to health and growth definitely involves spiritual warfare. As I have stated before, I believe our Lord is disappointed with his church in our nation while his archenemy is delighted. When it comes to the battle for souls, the church is losing by a landslide. A spiritual battle will be required to change this phenomenon, and those who take on this assault must be prepared.

Almost every denomination or association of congregations with whom I work tells me the same story. Their recent attempts to change have involved failed ministry program after failed ministry program. It is as though every year there is the program *de jour* that everyone is encouraged to implement with the assumption that these programs will produce revitalization and transformation. As the evidence attests, these programs, many of them quite good and valid, have not worked. I believe one major reason for their failure is that the assaults on dysfunction and death have been piecemeal, instead of a well-developed and thought-through strategy that takes advantage of all the resources available in order to win the battle. It's like pastors and congregations have been sent the newest rifle, machine gun, tank, or plane and are told that if they wield these weapons well they will win. In many cases pastors are not trained well in the use of the new programs. In almost all cases the new programs are not implemented in relation to an overall strategy designed to provide congregational transformation. We know today that to assault the gates with effectiveness means developing a strategy that takes advantage of all the resources that God puts at our disposal in order to win.

I believe the strategy must begin with and include prayer throughout its implementation. After all, this is a spiritual battle. The strategy must also take advantage of all the resources we have today that help us understand health, growth, and reproduction. The strategy must include pastors who are willing to become lifelong learners who will lead. It requires the deployment of dedicated lay leaders who will stand with mission-minded pastors and help the congregation move from stagnation to an outward-focused mission.

The denomination also must be willing to use its resources to help congregations turn around. The biggest resource the denomination has, after its effective pastors, is influence. In fact this influence can be more important than time or dollars. This influence needs to be used to make an unwavering commitment of support to the islands of health (congregations willing to make the difficult decisions required for health and growth) and a strong commitment of intentional neglect to the islands of disease (congregations unwilling to make the difficult decisions required for health and growth). The next biggest resource denominations have is the ability (now seldom used) to bring together highly effective pastors to work with other pastors, lay leaders, and congregations that want to become effective. The infrastructure is already in place; it just needs to be aligned correctly.

The major reason denominations need to implement this strategy is something I have addressed in other books. The average pastor is not a leader, either because of the lack of talent or the lack of gifting. This is not the pastor's problem, since this is the Creator's desire. Many pastors can exercise effective leadership behavior, however, if they have help. Pastors without the talent or gifting required to lead systemic transformation need someone to come alongside and stand with them. Denominations are built for such a task, although right now most people within denominations lack the knowledge or the courage to act as they need to in order for such transformation to take place. I know this situation can be remedied, though; I am seeing it happen in various denominational settings.

Pastors without the talent or gifting for leadership who work in independent congregations, or ones who act independently, are at a real disadvantage. They have no one to come and stand with them unless they hire someone from outside the congregation who is both able and willing to perform this task. Even then most change does not last because there is no sustainable mechanism to help the new DNA take root. Leaders in congregations that are part of denominations or associations of congregations should more readily be able to find the help they need—if denominations will do their part.

The Implementation

The route to congregational transformation, in order to create healthy parents for congregational reproduction, revolves around one grand strategy that includes three major initiatives. These three initiatives involve pastors, congregational units, and laity. Orchestrating this entire strategy is the role of the local judicatory, working in concert with the pastors, congregations, and lay leaders within congregations. The concept behind the strategy is one of layered learning, where people are forced to interact in a variety of ways with the same key concepts and behaviors. This strategy is also based upon the notion that in this day and age you must attract people to accountable relationships, understanding that you cannot compel them to be accountable. Without some strict accountability, though, systemic change will not occur.

This strategy allows local judicatories to engage in an experiment without having to make major changes (in most cases) to the way business is conducted daily. It provides a chance to see if change will occur—resulting in healthy, growing congregations—

without upsetting the denominational or associational structure. Implementing this strategy also allows the judicatory leaders to try something significant without looking foolish if it does not work. Trying a strategy with a handful of pastors and congregations as an experiment resolves the hesitancy judicatories now face in introducing new programs to all their pastors and congregations.

The Cluster/Learning Community Initiative

The first piece of the strategy is gathering a group of pastors into a cluster or learning community, meeting monthly for a minimum of one year, to learn about, discuss, and hold each other accountable for growth in the areas of leadership and congregational health. The cluster is based upon the development of a covenant where pastors and the denomination or association agree to behave in certain ways. This cluster, learning community, group, or gathering (in some denominations the word "cluster" has taken on negative meanings due to failures in the past in gathering pastors together for some purpose) is led by a current or former pastor who has had more success than any other pastor involved in the cluster in leading a congregation to grow primarily through evangelism. This leader of the group determines how the cluster will operate for the twelve or more months it meets. This is not a peer-led group, since such groups will never produce the accountable relationships required to lead systemic transformation.

The Consultation Initiative

As stated in *Direct Hit,* congregations on the upside of the life cycle often need consultations in order to achieve the next level of effectiveness. Congregations on the down side need an intervention. In this section we will talk more about congregations on the down side of their life cycles, which means that my descriptions will be more about interventions than consultations. However, even when we do interventions we call them consultations.

The consultation is the second initiative of the three-part strategy. Consultations involve two aspects. The first aspect is the weekend. The second aspect is walking alongside the congregation for a minimum of one year, coaching them to implement the changes resulting from the weekend part of the consultation. Those conducting the consultations and year-long coaching assignments are individuals who have led or are leading healthy, growing congregations larger in size than the church with which they are working.

The purpose of any consultation is twofold. First, one must deal with the proverbial elephants in the living room. This is true regardless of where a congregation is in its life cycle. However, if the congregation is on the down side the elephants are bigger and there are more of them. The second purpose is to offer the congregation hope by providing it a clear, specific, and detailed path that will lead to greater health and effectiveness as a result of the consultation.

The weekend usually reflects a clear, consistent pattern that becomes unique for each congregation based on their particular strengths and concerns. The report that is presented to the congregation at the end of the weekend generally lists the top five strengths of the congregation, the top five concerns or problems that are hindering health and growth, and five specific prescriptions. Each prescription is directed to one of the five concerns and states specific behaviors the congregation and its leaders need to implement within certain deadlines.

After listing each of these areas (strengths, concerns, and prescriptions), another date is given to the congregation. This date is normally four to six weeks following the actual weekend event. On that date the congregation is to vote (voting is crucial, regardless of the congregation's polity) to either embrace or reject the weekend consultation report in its entirety. Failure to vote or failure to embrace the entire report is seen as rejection. If the congregation votes to embrace the report, the judicatory or associational leaders commit to walking alongside the congregation for a minimum of one year to provide the needed resources to effectively implement the report. If the congregation rejects the report, the judicatory or associational leaders tell the congregation that they will not work with them in any intentional way to encourage health and effectiveness.

Once a congregation embraces the report, the judicatory or denominational leaders then promise to provide an effective congregational coach who will be on the campus of the congregation at least once a month for twelve months, helping the congregation make the changes spelled out in the report. They will also provide any resources (people, time, and in some cases money) required to make the needed changes.

This second initiative of the three-part strategy is where health and resulting growth begin to occur. It is the only process I know of where denominational people (who hopefully are well-trained to do this) roll up their sleeves and get involved in the life of the congregation. They first do it in an intense way on the weekend and then do it with regularity and consistency during the twelve months of coaching.

The Lay Leadership Training Initiative

During the year that the pastors are meeting in clusters or learning communities, and their respective congregations are experiencing consultations, the laity in the congregations are invited to two training events. The purpose of these events is to reinforce that which the pastors have been learning in their cluster meetings about healthy missional congregations. These training events also support all that is happening in the congregations as a result of the congregational consultations. The individuals conducting the training must have led, or be currently leading, a healthy, growing congregation larger than the congregations they are training.

The first training event focuses on a healthy congregation, what it looks like and how it behaves. The second training event focuses on making the mission of the Great Commission the primary value of the congregation.

The three-part strategy is a layered learning experience. The same ideas, concepts, and strategies that the pastors are learning each month in the cluster experience are communicated in an intense way in the consultation. The same issues are also communicated in the lay leadership training events.

The Role of the Judicatory or Association

The role of the judicatory or association is to attract pastors and congregations to the strategy. Once that occurs, the role then becomes one of overseeing the strategy and providing the resources to implement the strategy effectively. The key resource is getting the right cluster leaders, consultants, and congregational coaches, as well as the people leading the lay training events. Most judicatories and associations will need to realize that often the right people may not be in their denomination. This means they will, at times, need to look outside their denomination to find these leaders, until they have enough trained individuals to fill these key roles.

Assaulting the Gates

Like a great army preparing for war, the church of Jesus Christ needs to assemble its forces to assault the gates of the Evil One. That is what this strategy does. It prepares the leader pastors for their tasks. It focuses congregations on mission. It trains the lay leaders to march in sync with their pastors and the mission. The judicatory or association functions like the Pentagon, marshalling and training the right forces to perform the correct tasks. When groups of congregations exercise this strategy well, they see, on average, a 50 percent turnaround of the congregations involved in the process.

Developing the Strategy

In the following chapters I want to develop the strategy even further. First (chapter 2) I need to talk about what judicatories and associations need to do to implement the strategy. In most cases this strategy can be tried as a "research and development" experiment. It usually does not take many, if any, structural changes. However, there are some difficult decisions that someone needs to make initially and then see that they are carried out. Therefore, the issues involved need to be delineated.

Next (chapter 3) I want to talk about the cluster of pastors. Which pastors are selected? What do they covenant to do? What is taught for twelve months? These are some of the key questions that need to be addressed.

It will be important to spend two chapters (chapters 4 and 5) on the consultation, since the consultation is always in two parts—the weekend and the year of walking alongside a congregation. The two parts are quite different and accomplish different agendas. If both parts are implemented well, however, the congregation moves from maintenance to mission and begins to grow by making more disciples for Jesus Christ.

I then want to discuss in some detail in chapter 6 the lay leadership training. If the laity are not brought on board, then nothing will happen long-term. I am convinced that most laity want to see their congregations be healthy, effective, and growing. Many are tired of the "church bosses" running the show but do not know what to do. Once key laity are unleashed for mission, pastors will have great allies to help, in ways that are often beyond belief, in seeing congregations achieve God's vision in their communities.

It is important to discuss the roles of coaches, mentors, trainers, and consultants (see chapter 7). These key individuals are crucial resources that judicatories and associations need to both employ and develop if they are going to be involved in a sustained process of transformation.

Finally (in chapter 8), some judicatory and associational leaders will share how this strategy is working for them. These individuals will come from very diverse ecclesiastical traditions. God is working through a number of different traditions to add one more piece to the assault team. That piece involves pockets of denominational groups who are committed to the mission of making more and more disciples. These leaders are also adopting the Kingdom value of working together and sharing their new understandings with a wide variety of other denominational groups.

CHAPTER TWO
Flanking the Enemy

Donald serves his state bishop as the Director of Congregational Renewal. No one in his particular judicatory knows the state of the congregations like he does. Out of the 178 congregations, only ten have five hundred or more in worship, fifteen others have broken through the two-hundred barrier, and only 12 percent of all the congregations are growing. Most of the recent new church starts, of which there have been very few, are struggling to survive. The majority of congregations have fewer than one hundred in worship attendance.

Many of the pastors are discouraged and convinced that the current situation is not going to get better, and if anything will get worse. The pastors of the larger, growing congregations are doing their own thing and want little to do with the judicatory or even the other pastors. Most of the pastors are frustrated with the denomination, because each year it seems to have a new plan for growth that never works, and they feel the pressure from denominational leaders to generate more dollars for the denomination from an ever-decreasing funding base.

Donald is also highly frustrated. The effective pastors politely ignore him, while the rest look to him to help them survive the current morass in which they find themselves. His state bishop agrees the system is not working but does not have the funds to try something radically different nor the courage to change the systems. Most of the pastors are not interested in taking major risks, since they feel that doing so will put their vulnerable positions in even greater danger. Donald feels that he is living in a bad dream where he is called to repeat a "Catch-22" experience every day.

Donald decides to act, for his own sanity and for the kingdom of God. He begins to see if he can recruit his most effective pastors to help him implement a vision of change that is outside the normal denominational structure and behaviors. He finds one who is willing to meet monthly with pastors who are willing to learn about how to lead their congregations to health. However, this pastor says that he will not lead such a group if the members are unwilling to commit to reading, learning, and doing something with what they have learned. Donald affirms that he will recruit

only pastors who have the potential to lead change and who will commit to any accountability the pastor requires.

Donald then covertly redirects some budgeted funds he has at his disposal to engage an independent consultant to be the person who will come in and, in cooperation with the mentor pastor, actually work with the congregations of the mentor group of pastors. This consultant goes in and begins to both encourage and confront these congregations to follow their pastor in order to once again realize congregational health and experience growth. Donald, who is facing a major learning curve himself, works with both the pastor and the consultant to come alongside these congregations and provide continual networking and accountability to lead change.

After one year of working intensely with eight congregations, Donald sees five begin the initial phase of transformation. The five pastors are energized, the congregations are excited, the mentor pastor sees a broader Kingdom ministry he never thought he would have, and even the consultant is encouraged as he sees a better percentage of results than he normally experiences.

Donald now realizes that if this experience were repeated every year, within five years the state would see twenty-five to thirty more healthy congregations than it now has. If Donald could find just two more mentor pastors, that number could double or triple during the same period of time. And in the process no denominational structures have been altered or sacred cows sacrificed.

Uniqueness Is Sometimes a Curse

As I work with a multitude of denominations, I realize that my judicatory, Growing Healthy Churches (formerly the American Baptist Churches of the West), is unique. And often that uniqueness works against us as we try to serve and help other denominations realize the blessing of seeing an ever-expanding number of new disciples following Jesus Christ through the transformation of existing congregations and the launching of new ones. Therefore I first want to share with you what that uniqueness is and then articulate the problems this uniqueness creates for other denominations or associations of congregations.

Mission and Vision Driven

Our change started with a mission and a vision. The mission of the region was to help congregations transform. The vision was to see 70 percent of our congregations growing in five years. God blessed our region by allowing us to accomplish the mission and see the vision achieved.

In developing this mission and vision we began to act very differently from most denominational or associational entities. We saw each local congregation as having the same mission: to make disciples for Jesus Christ. Our role was to help them accomplish that mission. That meant that we would only work with those pastors and congregations that were willing to be committed to such a mission. In modern-day terms we decided to work with the islands of health (or those that were willing to become healthy) and not work with the islands of disease (particularly the ones that desired to remain sick).

Another implication of this decision was to work with our national body when its mission fit ours and the mission we believed local congregations were called to fulfill. At the same time, it also meant that we would not support any national agenda or initiative that worked against our mission or that of our congregations. Obviously, this decision created problems at the local, regional, and national levels. Despite this, we believe that God protected us and enabled us to remain effective in doing what we were convinced God had called us to do.

The result of God blessing our region with many healthy, growing, "Great Commission" congregations convinced us to remain faithful to our mission and then create a new vision (since the first had been achieved) that was consistent with that mission. The new vision meant that the focus of our region broadened beyond transformation (which we still do, because transformation is a continuing process) to include reproduction. Again, God's blessing of starting many new, larger congregations has convinced us that we must be driven by our mission and vision.

Thus we constantly lead the region and evaluate our decisions and behaviors in light of the mission and vision, rather than traditions, structures, or religious and business policy manuals. We tend to ignore the whims of denominational loyalists who still believe the franchise model is working and somehow think that God has given their denomination some special insight in how to act or a reason to exist.

Selling our camps (even though one of the two was still profitable), changing our name (from ABCW to GHC), developing new streams of income, developing staff accountability—these are all missional decisions. These choices now allow us to move quickly while exploring new initiatives without normal organizational and denominational constraints. We have endured the battles with those who want us to be and act differently and no longer hear the complaints from those who would rather maintain the status quo than risk institutional and traditional values in order to become effective. All of these things make our region quite distinct. We have moved to the middle ground between a denominational entity and a full-fledged network, functioning much more like a network than an institution.

A Structure That Supports Mission and Vision

We now have a structure based on the Accountable Leadership Model developed by John Kaiser. This structure marries responsibility, authority, and accountability, as it is supposed to do. Those who direct ministries are given the freedom to lead their areas as they see fit while being held accountable for goals. The value of "faithfulness" has not been lost, while the value of "fruitfulness" has been added.

This means that there are few organizational meetings. Rather, individuals develop their teams to assist them. The teams make the decisions and carry out the ministry. The major purpose of meetings is for integrating strategy, keeping everyone up-to-date, and developing synergy between respective ministry areas. This means that meetings are called for ministry purposes and are only held when required. They tend to be short and formalities are often ignored, particularly when they get in the way of achieving goals. My staff and I attend very few meetings each year since we simply do not meet that often.

Our meetings have been replaced with training sessions. Pastors meet in groups regularly for training. Almost all of our regional meetings are for training, with special training sessions called when opportunities for exposure to effective people and their ideas becomes available.

The Seven Values

Being structured around the mission and vision allows GHC to actually live out its values. Many organizations, including congregations, have stated values. Too often, though, these are simply lists of wishes of how people within the entity should act but often fail to because the structure and real values will not let them. All mission and vision-driven organizations find much closer consistency between their stated values and their actual behaviors. We find that the consistent implementation of our values pushes us in the direction of moving from being a denominational entity to acting much more like a network.

Laser Focus on the Great Commission

As I have stated previously, we believe that every congregation has the same mission: to make more disciples for Jesus Christ. We believe that every congregation needs to be held accountable for consistently making new disciples (both children and adults) every year. I am convinced that mission forms the basis of all congregational health, and that the congregation's mission is to change its community by regularly and consistently seeing new disciples enter into an eternal relationship with God through faith in Jesus Christ. Congregations that fail to do this are not only unhealthy, they are disobedient. They are not meeting the purpose that the Lord of the church instituted his church to accomplish. The good news is that when congregations admit their collective sin and ask forgiveness, God not only forgives but begins to help them change their ways. Our commitment to this mission is grounded in our theology. The implementation of the mission produces congregational health and reproduction.

Congregational Health Produces Growth

In God's creative order all living things that are healthy grow and reproduce. The same is true for God's church, which is a living organism. God said it would grow and therefore expects it to grow.

Any congregation will grow when it is healthy, regardless of its location. This means that congregations that are not growing through making new disciples are sick. Such congregations must be confronted about such lack of health. These congregations must then be taught how to address the issues that contribute to their illness, while also addressing those ideas that will bring health. We do know what it takes to lead a congregation from sickness to health. We can offer them that hope. For that hope to be eternally effective, it demands the congregation trust that God will respond and produce growth, as it moves from sickness to health. The issue is not the size of the congregation. The issue is health, since health produces growth and eventual reproduction.

Ruthless Accountablity

No real change occurs without accountablity measures being put into place. The reasons most congregations do not turn around and the reason most denominations will not turn around is that professional clergy tend to run from accountability like animals fleeing a forest fire. Yet without an accountability that has teeth to it there will be no change. In GHC I am held accountable, and I keep my position based upon the achievement of specific and measurable goals that have been approved by our corporate board. While I am given great freedom in how to accomplish those goals, I am evaluated based on whether or not the goals are achieved. Many of our pastors have entered into an accountability relationship with their church boards or councils for the achievement of goals. A good number of pastors have also allowed us at the judicatory level to be another entity that holds them accountable. These pastors, along with congregational leaders, understand that an accountability system outside their congregation can be highly beneficial.

We also function this way with our congregations. Those congregations that are the islands of health (those seeking to grow by regularly and consistently making new disciples) receive the focus of our resources. Those not seeking to follow the Great Commission with rigor do not. Those congregations unwilling to make the Great Commission the value that drives all congregational behavior do not have access to many of the resources available to congregations committed to fulfilling the Great Commission.

God Expects Shepherds to Lead

Shepherds are entrepreneurs who lead sheep into green pastures and by still waters in order to eventually shear them, get them to reproduce, and kill them. Such actions demand that shepherds be leaders, not chaplains. GHC has focused on leadership, leadership, and more leadership for more than a decade. We ask those pastors who do not have either the gift or the talent for leadership to exercise learned leadership behavior. We believe that pastors need to continually develop their leadership behavioral skills. These pastors also need to be recruiting and developing lay leaders who in turn will recruit and develop more leaders. Pastors are expected to train their staff and board members and other people in groups they have recruited as future leaders in the congregation.

God Expects Congregations to Influence Their Communities

We believe that large congregations are a cultural mandate. We live in a culture where influence is related to size. We respect, shop, and participate in large stores and institutions. Because we do, they have influence over us and our society. This is even true for those ubiquitous boutique coffee shops. We may value their small feel, but we want them to be located wherever we are in order to get our latte fix when needed.

Larger congregations are able to influence communities for the gospel and for Jesus Christ. We believe that pastors are called to pastor their community, not just their congregation. They need to be leaders who speak to the life of the community and are heard and respected. Such hearing and respect is often in proportion to the size of their congregation and the sphere of ministry that congregation has in the community.

The Church of Jesus Christ Is a Missional Entity

We believe God did not design the church of Jesus Christ for Christians. Rather, we believe that God designed the church to mobilize Christians to attack the gates of hell. In other words, the church is not to be a place of safety for believers but rather a gathering place to accomplish mission. This is the biggest issue facing the church of Jesus Christ in the United States and in cultures similar to the United States. Most Christians believe their congregations exist for them. We believe the opposite, which is the main reason so many of our congregations are outward in their orientation.

If our belief is correct, then the church is a missional entity. If it is a missional entity, then many of the issues Christians fight over go out the window. Who cares about the genre of music being sung if it accomplishes the mission? Who cares when and how we meet if the mission is being accomplished? Who cares how we are structured if the mission is being accomplished? And who cares about our denominational label if the mission is being accomplished?

If each congregation is a missional entity, then each pastor is ultimately a missionary. Missionaries become amateur students of the culture. They then work to remove those cultural barriers that hinder people from hearing the gospel. They also build cultural bridges that help people meet the God of the Bible, who created cultures, through faith in the living, resurrected Jesus Christ. Missional pastors are constantly leveraging a smaller group (the congregation) to influence a larger group (the community in which the congregation exists).

The Bottom Line Is Reproduction

All believers, groups of believers (congregations), and groups of congregations (denominations and associations) are to be reproducing. I raised my children to leave home. My hope (which has been fulfilled) was that they would marry someone and produce exceptional grandchildren. Physical maturity is defined by reproduction—as is spiritual maturity. Spiritually mature believers are those who are involved in the process of making new disciples. Spiritually mature congregations are those involved in reproducing. The reproduction for congregations may start with multiple services, moving then to multiple venues, and then eventually to separate congregations. Spiritually mature denominations are consistently involved in the reproduction of new congregations. The ultimate goal for every healthy congregation and denomination is to reproduce new disciples individually and groups of new disciples—new congregations.

The Big Question

The Conundrum

Almost all of the judicatories and associations of congregations I work with marvel at the way we function. Many cannot believe that GHC functions as simply and freely as it does. A good number of people say they wish their entity would function like ours. But when it comes to making the decisions to function and act like we do, almost all lack either the courage or the institutional leeway to make it happen. It is much easier for the less connectional groups to accomplish that which God has created in our region. Even there, however, in most cases no one is strong enough or capable enough to lead such change. And those who do have the ability often do not want to pay the price required to make it happen. In the more connectional denominations there are usually layers above the middle judicatory that would stop or hinder the kinds of changes we have implemented. Yet all these groups want the results God, in his grace, is still allowing us to see. Therefore the question I constantly get is: *Is it possible to see God bless many of our congregations with health and growth without becoming GHC?*

The Answer

The answer is now a resounding yes. I have been testing a strategy with a number of denominations to see if it is possible to bring consistent transformation to congregations that are on a plateau or in decline, without implementing the organizational and denominational changes we adopted.

What is required is that each judicatory be willing to let a handful of congregations enter into a research and design experiment for a period of time (usually at least three years). In the more connectional groups this may mean suspending some of the normal traditions that are part of that group's customary way of doing business. For example, in denominations where bishops or others have the ability to move pastors, those pastors and congregations in the experiment are promised that the pastors will not be moved while the experiment is being implemented. In the less connectional groups it may simply be getting congregations and pastors to volunteer for the experiment and then organizing and funding the experiment as required.

While this experiment does not require a denomination to make all the changes GHC has made, it does include within its parts the seven values that reflect the behaviors of GHC. Obviously, some changes are required in order to practice the behaviors demanded by the values intrinsic to the strategy being proposed. However, systemic changes involving denominational or associational structures do not have to occur.

The groups who have implemented this strategy properly have seen a minimum of 50 percent of the congregations involved in the experiment experience significant transformation.

Key Assumptions Underlying the Strategy

The Leader

Although the judicatory or association of congregations does not need to go through the systemic changes experienced by GHC, there must be someone in the group of congregations who has the desire and the ability both to sell the experiment to others and then to see that it happens. If the leader of the judicatory is not the one generating the experiment, then it must be someone that leader respects enough in order to give them a chance to make it happen. Seldom will this experiment work if it is instigated by a person like a consultant, who is tangential to the judicatory or association. If, however, the consultant is brought in by the judicatory leader and given the authority to conduct the experiment, it can work.

The person instigating the experiment also must have some leverage with the pastors and lay leaders in the judicatory or association. Such leverage is important because this person must both create urgency for trying the experiment and cast vision about what the experiment will accomplish. This person must also have the relationships and ability to recruit the pastors and convince lay leaders and congregations to participate.

The Rate of Change

The situations faced by denominations and congregations in our country did not happen overnight. The decline in congregations, new disciples, dollars, judicatories, and denominations has been going on for decades. Therefore there is no quick fix. Any denominational entity is changed one congregation at a time. Failure to grasp this concept has been the problem for denominations in the recent past. Every year a new program for change has been presented to the pastors and congregations. When it has not worked or worked well in a relatively short period of time, it has been jettisoned for the next quick fix. Denominational leaders must understand that no quick fixes exist.

It also means that no one program will work. What is required for change is an overall strategy that involves pastors, lay leaders, congregations, and the denomination itself in order to work. Everyone must be involved. The assault only works when all the resources are aligned for victory. The good news about this strategy is that it does involve everyone without requiring up front the changes that the denomination will have to encounter some day in order to be what God intended them to be and what they once were. However, those changes will be easier to make when they are led by effective pastors in healthy congregations rather than by ineffective pastors in highly toxic congregations.

Attracted to Accountability

Accountability is required for change, as I have already stated. In our culture, however, regardless of polity, no one can be forced into accountable relationships when they have not existed prior to adopting the new. If people are forced to be accountable, all they will do is check off the items on the list without producing real change.

Therefore, for an accountable model to work, the accountability process must be something that people are invited to participate in and are therefore willing to try because they believe in and value the benefits that will occur as a result. They also must be convinced that all the other people submitting to the model are being held accountable on the same basis as themselves. Finally, they need to realize that the purpose of accountability is not to penalize and weed people out (although that may happen eventually) but rather that accountability is required to produce significant fruit for the kingdom of God.

Change and Pain

Change will not occur in any dying organization without pain. The question is whether the rate of pain will be gradual, as is happening in most denominations (slow death), or whether the rate will be more instantaneous and therefore the change more significant. This means that the congregations involved in the experiment will feel far more significant pain than the denomination in which the pain is being experienced slowly and gradually. If the congregations do not feel such pain, then real change is not occurring.

Those overseeing the judicatory or association of congregations must understand that such pain will occur, must be willing to tolerate it, and must handle it correctly. It will mean standing with the pastors and lay leaders that are the focus of the change. It also means recognizing that in many cases congregations will need to lose people before they can gain people—but that when they do gain members, it will be many more than they lost. The denomination needs to understand that those initial losses may result in financial costs as the budgets of the congregations going through such change will be impacted negatively. The negative impact in congregational budgets will result in a negative impact on judicatory budgets. Our region gained a 25 percent increase in mission dollars over a period of five years. Yet there were times during those five years when we struggled with our regional budget while congregations lost some of their givers. Ultimately, the growth of new people in congregations that were now healthy and growing more than made up for the losses that we initially sustained.

Judicatories struggling with a lack of funds (since congregations are declining) will eventually benefit. However, if money or institutional survival are the reasons for implementing this strategy, the experiment will not work. Not only are these motivations ungodly, they will eventually become apparent. The result will be a loss of morale and commitment to making the experiment work among the participants. The motivation for trying this experiment must be to see a continual stream of new disciples entering into the kingdom of God through the efforts of healthy congregations.

Truth and Hope

Bringing change to sick and highly dysfunctional organizations (a description that fits many congregations) requires telling the truth while offering hope. Telling the truth means addressing those issues that are the causes of decline and ineffectiveness. Sometimes this truth telling includes looking congregational "power brokers" in the eye and letting them know that they must either change or be removed from their positions of influence. Truth telling is often not easy and is many times unpleasant, yet it must happen if there is to be systemic change. Those in the judicatory or association must understand that often the pain they will hear about or experience is coming from long-time, denominational-stalwart members who are being removed from power in their congregations. Such people will expect the denomination to come to their aid out of regard for their years of faithful attendance and giving. To support these people in their complaint will doom the experiment to failure. It is essential that judicatory leaders stand firm at this point, regardless of how many e-mails or phone calls they receive. Backing down will undermine the entire effort.

While truth-telling is hard and unpleasant work, it is not the toughest task. The more difficult task is offering small, dying, older, and hopeless congregations hope. Hope comes when people not only tell them there can be a better day but know how to actually teach the congregation to make this better day become a reality. Hope means knowing what it takes to see a congregation become healthy, so that if God wants this congregation to grow it has the means to do so. If this hope cannot be offered, then again the experiment will not work. The experiment will simply become another failed program of the denomination. That is why those working with congregations must have the experience of having led churches to health and effectiveness. This is not the time to prescribe behaviors based only on theory derived from books or seminars.

Leading from Experience

A key leadership concept that contributed significantly to the turnaround of our congregations was that the leader always led from experience, not simply potential. This means that those who train, consult, coach, and mentor have already done that which they are working to help others achieve. The same is true in this experiment. Those leading and implementing the experiment must have already achieved that which they are leading others to accomplish.

This concept is perhaps the hardest one for denominations to implement. One major reason that most denominations are in the state they are in is that the majority of people in positions of leadership at all levels have seldom led a larger, healthy, growing congregation. They do not know what to do—they are always speaking from theory, not practice.

For this reason many judicatories will need to outsource all or parts of the experiment. I am working with one denomination currently that is seeing some good turnaround in a very short amount of time. Many of the pieces in the experiment, though, are being led by people who are not part of the denomination.

Independent Congregations

Some of those reading this book may well belong to congregations that have no relationship with either a denomination or association of congregations. Perhaps your congregation has been independent since its inception, or, as is often the case, at some point in its history it left a denomination. You may be wondering how this experiment could work for you.

First let me say that there are clear advantages to not being a part of a denomination. The key advantage is that you are not bound to a communal anchor that often provides little or no help in transforming your congregation or leading it to reproduction while taking money for denominational efforts of limited or no benefit to your congregation. Further, you are not tainted with the bigger denominational issues that hit the news media and reflect badly on the testimony of Jesus Christ and your efforts to do mission in your community. The disadvantage, of course, is that if a judicatory or association becomes serious about transformation and reproduction and is either doing it well or trying an experiment like the one described in this book, you cannot take advantage of such a resource. When a judicatory or association is serious about helping congregations transform and reproduce, the benefits of membership in the denomination are well worth the costs.

It seems to me that independent congregations have two options. The first option is to join a shadow denomination like the ones run by many of the megachurches in the nation. The number of megachurches in the U.S. has doubled in the last five years, and many of them provide some kind of resources for other local congregations. When you join these megachurch associations, however, let them know that you are interested in more than attending conferences and getting CDs and books. Tell them you want them to develop some kind of strategy that enables the leaders to bring their expertise to your congregation in order to help it transform and become involved in continual reproduction.

The second option is to contact consultants, mentors, and coaches who know what they are doing and hire the expertise you need in order to get the job accomplished. This is the more expensive way to go, and you run the risk of the congregation not respecting the consultant, since it was the pastor or some key leader who instigated all this trouble. If you do not have a group with which you are connected that can help you, however, then it seems to me that this is your only option.

Summary

Many congregations, judicatories, denominations, and associations of congregations want God to do for them what God in his grace has done for many of the congregations of GHC. They want to see systemic transformation that leads to health, growth, the making of new disciples, and eventually congregational reproduction. Yet many congregations are in denominational settings that, for a variety of reasons, will not allow such growth to occur. Also, many denominational leaders who want the best for their congregations are not sure they either want or have the ability to lead the denominational changes we have made in GHC. Therefore, the question is whether they can see change in their congregations without going through all the other changes. The answer is yes they can. We have developed a strategy that, if followed well, will witness significant turnaround in at least 50 percent of the participating congregations.

This strategy demands the understanding of certain assumptions and is based on some basic values upon which GHC functions. And, if followed, using the right kind of experienced leaders, it works.

CHAPTER THREE
Recruiting the Officers

Strategy One: The Cluster Initiative

Bill was a frustrated leader. While in seminary he had taken on leadership of a congregation as a pastoral intern. During the five years he was there as the pastor, he had graduated from seminary, seen the church grow up to the 200 barrier, and been involved in creating significant ministry initiatives in his community. He then left that congregation to pastor one that was much larger. The first five years in his new congregation, however, saw little if any growth. He had led this congregation to root out people with inappropriate lifestyles from leadership positions. The congregation, which in the past had been three times its current size, was ready to begin renovation of its facilities. For his part, Bill felt he was just spinning his wheels. He wondered if this was all that the rest of his pastoral ministry had in store for him.

His judicatory leader came to him and asked if he would be in a cluster of pastors that would meet monthly for twelve months. The purpose of the cluster was to provide training in the areas of leadership and congregational health. If Bill became involved he would need to be open to having a congregational consultation and also to getting his lay leaders to attend some training events designed for his church.

The judicatory leader wanted Bill in the cluster; most of the other pastors looked up to Bill because his congregation was much larger than theirs. He knew that it would be easier to recruit others if he could tell them that Bill would be there. Bill was interested in being part of the group because of where he was in ministry and what was not happening in the congregation he was leading. Therefore he agreed to join.

Bill attended every meeting but one (which he missed due to a commitment made before the schedule was established). He participated enthusiastically, and his leadership in reading the books and completing the assignments provided encouragement for the other pastors in the group. He was also very open and vulnerable about what he was dealing with, what he was thinking, and what displeased him about ministry, even though most of the pastors in the group thought that he must have it all together since his congregation was so much larger than theirs.

Bill recruited his lay leaders to attend the training and participated fully in the consultation process. Bill will tell you today that not only has this experience changed his life, energized his ministry, and caused his congregation to grow significantly; it has ultimately saved his commitment to vocational ministry. More than just an effective pastor, today Bill is a leader in his judicatory, coaching and mentoring other pastors to achieve health and growth in their congregations.

Introduction

The first part of the strategy begins with the pastors. This piece of the strategy includes the selection, recruitment, and training of pastors to lead congregational transformation. Our church culture still sees the pastor in a position of leadership, even if often the pastor is expected to act more like a chaplain than a leader. The simple fact that people come each week to hear her or him speak means that the pastor is in a position to lead, regardless of whether or not she or he takes advantage of this position or is allowed to lead by congregational leaders. If everything rises and falls in relation to leadership, then any strategy for turnaround must begin with those who are in a position to lead. We also found in our turnaround situations that the ability to experience transformation and eventual reproduction depends on the pastor's ability to lead the congregation.

My recommendation to judicatories or associations employing the experiment is that they begin with one or no more than two pastoral groupings or clusters. I also recommend that there be a minimum of five and a maximum of ten pastors in each group. With five pastors in a group, you still have at least four to work with if one drops out for some reason. Having more than ten makes it difficult to achieve the dynamics you want to occur in the group meetings. Also, the group meeting is for either solo pastors or senior pastors, not other staff members. This means that each pastor in the group represents one congregation. Also, pastors with staff members usually feel much freer to share staffing issues that may be hindering growth if only solo or senior pastors are involved.

Recruiting Pastors

Once a judicatory decides to implement the strategy, the first question asked is usually how to recruit pastors for the first one or two clusters. The question is a crucial one. Any new initiative or strategy needs to have key early victories in order to gain acceptance by others and achieve momentum within the organization. Therefore, who is picked and how they are selected is key. I also realize that each organizational entity must deal with a variety of circumstances, including the context of local political concerns. Therefore, I am going to provide ideal options regarding the basic question of recruitment. Any adjustments need to remain as close to the ideals as possible.

The best way to begin is to share the strategy with the entire judicatory, to see if there is enough backing from leaders to implement it. However, the strategy needs to be communicated in the context of both urgency and vision. The urgency comes from the current state of the judicatory, the denomination, or the association of congregations. The strategy is then offered as a way of providing hope to see actual change occur, both to individual congregations as well as to the larger group in the long run. In this way the strategy itself becomes part of the vision.

As pastors, lay leaders, and congregations begin to learn about the new strategy and begin to ask questions about their possible involvement, the judicatory then tells them that there is a form to complete in order to possibly be selected to be part of this new experiment. It is important to let everyone know that the first one or two groups are like the guinea pigs in a scientific test. They will be used to test the way for others, who may not be a part of the group(s) this year but will probably be part of another new group next year. Presenting the strategy this way helps deal with feelings of hurt or loss that may come when pastors and congregations are not picked for the initial group(s).

If the strategy is presented well, it is best to have both the pastor and the congregational leaders apply to be part of the experiment. This creates initial "buy-in" at both the clergy and lay levels. If that is not possible, then simply work with the pastors to get their participation.

A second way to go about the recruitment of pastors and congregations is to simply invite those you want to participate. This method usually requires having someone on the judicatory staff who has both a passion for change and a good knowledge of those pastors who have the potential to be effective and whose congregations will be receptive to the behaviors required in the strategy. This is how we did it initially in our region. Later, as we were working with those we had recruited, I was sometimes asked by other pastors why they were not selected for that first year. My response was that I could only fill ten spots, and those selected understood they were "guinea pigs," since we were trying out a number of new ideas. If all of this worked I would start another group next year, inviting them to be a part of it, and they would participate knowing they were getting a better model of ministry as a result of what we were learning this year. The explanation worked. The strategy being laid out in this book has now evolved over a decade as we learn new things each time we implement it.

For those pastors who want this experience but are not selected for the first group, I would set out criteria for being selected in the next "go round" of clusters. In my book *Direct Hit* I lay out five things that pastors should be doing to prepare the congregation for change:

- Develop a prayer team that prays for: vision, the community, and new disciples.
- Develop a dream team that begins work on: vision and strategy.
- Develop a team of leaders who will: help you lead change at the appropriate time.
- Create an urgency calendar. Communicate urgency 52 Sundays a year.
- Create a vision calendar. Cast vision 52 Sundays a year.

Pastors not selected will be told that their ability to implement these five concepts and demonstrate how they have been implemented well will determine whether they are selected for the second year of pastoral groupings. If pastors are doing this already, the changes that will come in the implementation of the strategy will occur with more ease, since these five things are already part of the congregation's life. These five steps prepare a congregation well for systemic change.

Following the question of *how* pastors will be selected is always the question of *who* will be chosen. This is a key question, since it relates to both the changes in congregations and eventual change for the denomination. The result here is more important than the process; focus more on ending up with the right people than on how you go about getting them. Choosing the right pastors ensures both congregational change and the creation of momentum that will lead to more congregations being open to change and the transformation of the judicatory.

The determining human factor for success is the pastor, not the congregation. In other words, the pastor's ability to either be a leader or practice leadership behavior well trumps even the congregation's willingness to embrace change. Even the most recalcitrant congregation can be led through change if the right things happen and the right leader is in place. On the other hand, the congregation most eager for change and willing to be led will see little or no results if the wrong person is leading it.

Having said this, let me add that the first cluster should not have only naturally gifted leaders, nor contain only the congregations that are already changing or growing. If either or both of these factors occur, the other pastors and congregations not involved in the first year will believe (rightly so) that the deck was stacked and change occurred only because the right pastors with the better congregations were chosen. And as a result they will not be willing to sign up for the next group of clusters. This is a strategy that produces transformation for both pastors and congregations—meaning that there can be no doubt that genuine transformation has occurred in this first group.

If there are ten pastors in the first cluster, then I only want at most two or three who are leaders and whose congregations are larger, growing, or only recently hit a plateau. However, I definitely want a couple of pastors like this in the cluster if the judicatory has such pastors and can recruit them to participate. The reason is that under the cluster mentor's influence, these pastors will help lead the cluster and be a real source of both help and encouragement for the other participating pastors. These leaders among the first cluster participants (along with their churches) will benefit immensely from the experiment, and will be a great resource to the other pastors in the group.

The rest of the pastors need to be people that you and others believe can exercise leadership behavior well, even if they do not have the gift or talent of leadership. Also, I am assuming that none of these pastors will have growing congregations. There should be no more than three growing congregations represented in the cluster (remember the purpose of the strategy is to demonstrate transformation)! I do not care how old the pastors or congregations are or the size of each congregation's worship attendance. In fact, I would prefer to have quite a variety of congregational sizes represented if such is possible. The reason for this is that pastors in varying sizes of congregations can be of help to those who are leading congregations that are somewhat smaller than their own congregation. A good mix like this helps to generate peer learning in the cluster.

Sometimes it is easier to describe who should *not* be in the cluster. Do not put pastors in the cluster for whom you see this experience as their last chance to make it. Such pastors need to be held out until the second or third round, after you have achieved a good number of early victories. Also, do not put pastors in the cluster who are dealing with major character or professional issues. The purpose of the cluster is not counseling. The purpose is mentoring in order to help them grow and develop as effective pastors. Do not put into the cluster those pastors who have been around long enough to inherit the larger congregations that are not declining simply because they are the "flagship" churches of the denomination in the area. This is particularly important if these pastors act as though they have all the answers while in reality they have stopped learning. (There is often great denominational pressure to have such pastors in the cluster. However, they will do nothing but disrupt it.)

Finally, do not select pastors with marginal leadership behavior ability who are in highly conflicted or very small congregations (10-30) because you hope that this strategy will deal with those congregations. This is particularly true if you believe that the pastor should not be in vocational ministry or that the congregation needs to die. If you want the strategy to succeed, deal with these issues directly and do not use this strategy to address them. Deal with congregations like this separately, preferably later when you have a number of healthy, transformed congregations and pastors with newly acquired skills at congregational turnaround.

To summarize, then: don't stack the deck in the first group, but do select strategically, so the experiment will succeed.

The Cluster Mentor

The cluster leader should be a pastor within the denomination whose congregation is larger than anyone's in the cluster, and whose church is growing through consistently making new disciples of Jesus Christ. Only use a member of judicatory staff if he or she has recently pastored a congregation that meets these criteria. Otherwise, he or she should serve as the cluster facilitator, the person who makes sure that things occur in order to accomplish the strategy. If no pastor from your denomination who meets the above criteria is available, then outsource that role to an effective pastor from another denomination.

The cluster mentor (the one conducting the training) must have more experience than those being trained (the pastors in the cluster). However, the mentor must also understand that how they have conducted ministry, no matter how successfully, is not the only way that effective ministry can be accomplished. This person needs to know and be able to show how effective ministry may be accomplished in a variety of ways. They also need to be able to communicate these ideas well. In other words, they should be good trainers who are not just telling pastors to "do it the way I did it" but can show them principles and then help them develop a variety of strategies and tactics that reflect well the implementation of those principles. Good cluster mentors share a variety of ways that effective pastors address different issues or solve a myriad of common problems.

The cluster mentor's task is to train in two major areas: leadership and congregational health. The mentor needs to help pastors understand that they are to be leaders, show them what real pastoral leadership looks like, and explain the behaviors required to be such a leader. They also need to be teaching pastors what they must actually do to help their congregations become healthy in order to grow. If these mentors cannot cover that in every area of congregational life, they need to expose those in the cluster to the resources that will teach them. No one knows everything. There will be times when the mentor acts as a broker, connecting the pastors to the resources they need in order to be leaders and conduct congregational ministry effectively. At times the cluster mentor may invite other effective pastors to come into the cluster and provide training for a particular area of ministry.

The Covenant

A covenant is drawn up at the first meeting of the cluster. The purpose of the covenant is to develop an agreement between the pastors themselves, and the pastors and the judicatory, about what will be expected from each during the twelve months the cluster meets.

Pastors agree to attend all the meetings (at the first meeting everyone brings their calendars so all the dates for the twelve months can be established so no one misses due to vacations, conferences, etc.). They also agree to arrive on time and stay for the entire time (the latter is key, since pastors are notorious for leaving meetings early). The pastors agree to do any required reading (there is at least one book per month) and any other assignments given them by the cluster mentor.

The pastors also agree to participate in the entire strategy. This means that a consultation will be conducted for each congregation represented. It also means that pastors promise to recruit as many of their lay people as possible to attend the two training events that will be conducted during the first year. Pastors also agree to submit congregational statistics each month to the judicatory office. The statistics for each congregation will be distributed to every pastor in the cluster each month. (This agreement not only contributes to accountability but eventually creates interdependence among pastors as everyone begins to see that each congregation does some things well and other things need improvement.)

Pastors also covenant to pray for each other in their private devotions and to pray each Sunday for at least one pastor and congregation in the cluster.

The judicatory leaders covenant to do whatever it takes to support the pastors and the congregations as they implement the strategy. This means providing the resources for the cluster, the consultations, and the lay training events.

The completed covenant is given to all the pastors at the second cluster meeting. Each pastor is asked to sign a common copy so that all their signatures are on one copy of the covenant.

The covenant then becomes the basis for interacting with pastors and congregations that find difficulty implementing different parts of the strategy. This is why it is beneficial to include lay boards or councils in the process of recruiting pastors and their respective congregations for the first cluster. It is ideal to have both the pastors and then respective lay leadership groups sign off on the covenants. These groups are invited to interact in the creation of the cluster, but they should not be allowed to interfere with the essential elements of the strategy that are part of the covenant agreement.

The Cluster Meeting

Each cluster meeting lasts for a minimum of five hours, usually beginning at 9 a.m. and continuing to 2 p.m. The first three hours are led by the cluster mentor. This person's primary responsibility is to train the participants in the two areas of leadership and congregational health. After an opening prayer, the cluster leader usually interacts with the pastors over any book they had been asked to read and any assignment they had been asked to complete. All books and assignments should be related to leadership or congregational health. Therefore, interaction about the books involves discussion in the two key areas. After this interaction, the cluster mentor should conduct some kind of training related to either being and acting like a leader or understanding and implementing some area of congregational life that will produce health. The mentor should induce the pastors to interact in relation to their respective congregations and the situations in which they lead. It is good if the mentor can help pastors discuss particular situations related to the training being provided. Other pastors who have dealt well with similar situations can enter into the discussion at this point.

As congregations begin to have their consultations, time should be given for that pastor to react and discuss what happened during the weekend consultation and what has occurred in the congregation and with the leaders since the initial part of the consultation. These discussions provide great learning for all the pastors involved.

There is no one set curriculum for a cluster. Each one takes on a different form. New books on leadership and congregational health are constantly being published and becoming part of the list of required reading. Every congregation and pastor is different, so their individuality brings nuances to each cluster meeting. Each congregational consultation raises unique issues in both the life of the pastor and that of the congregation. Therefore, the cluster mentor needs to realize that flexibility is a key in providing the training.

The training must not become sidetracked, however. Pastors need to be forced to deal with issues, whether they are personal or ones related to congregational behavior. Also, individual spiritual issues and group bonding needs should be addressed in what occurs after lunch, following the three hours of training in leadership and congregational health.

The period after lunch should focus on spiritual formation issues. This is where the mentor may want to deal with more personal issues that have surfaced with pastors, for example, pastors working too may hours or not enough hours, relationships with spouses or children, and the like. This is to be a time for both corporate and individual worship and prayer. I do recommend a time when the mentor and judicatory person leaves and pastors form their own prayer groups and pray for each other. In fact, I highly recommend that pastors meet at another time each month but in the same group and share prayer requests for their individual needs, family needs, and ministry needs. Others should not be there so as to encourage vulnerability (that might not be achieved if others are present who may at some point have influence over ministry positions.

As these pastors lead systemic change, they will face greater opposition than they have ever faced before in their ministries. Moving congregations from an inward to an outward focus is a major spiritual endeavor that confronts the Evil One's control of the congregation. For that reason, the problems will sometimes be awesome, personal, and beyond comprehension. Thus, the time after lunch is crucial; it provides the emotional, psychological, and spiritual sustenance that many pastors will need.

Likewise, the three hours each morning spent on leadership and congregational health also must not be compromised. Without this training, most of the pastors involved will not know what to do and how to do it. These are two topics most pastors have never learned—they are usually not taught in seminary, and if taught are not taught well. Most denominations never teach in these areas because they cannot. And what is being taught each month should be implemented almost immediately, or at least in the near future.

Someone from the judicatory needs to attend each cluster meeting. This person facilitates the entire cluster event, freeing up the cluster mentor to provide training and lead spiritual formation.

This person handles all logistical issues relating to the meeting place, meals and coffee breaks, and any supplies required for the training. This individual produces and distributes copies of the covenant, statistical reports, books for next month's meeting, and any other items the judicatory is committed to produce for pastors and the cluster mentor.

The facilitator acts as a liaison between the cluster mentor, the pastors, and the judicatory. As facilitator, this person coordinates dates for consultations and lay training events. The facilitator also makes sure to meet any needs encountered by the cluster mentor in order to ensure that training occurs with excellence.

The facilitator plays a key role in serving the needs of all the parties involved. The bottom line for such a person is to see that the entire cluster event goes well.

Summary

Pastoral groupings or clusters are the first part of the three-part, layered learning strategy being communicated in this book. A group of pastors (usually no more than ten) are recruited to meet once each month for twelve months. The trainer of this group, the cluster mentor, is someone who has lead an effective, healthy, growing congregation that is or was larger than any represented in the cluster.

The pastors and the judicatory sponsoring the cluster create and sign a covenant that lays out the responsibilities each will fulfill. The pastors meet once a month for five hours. The first three hours are spent in learning about leadership and congregational health. The time after lunch is spent on spiritual formation issues.

The purpose is to develop pastors who will exercise leadership behavior in leading their congregations through transformation. This format also provides a great support system as pastors encounter difficulties in the transformation process.

Over the years these clusters have been the lifeline God has used to help pastors get through the trauma that is created when leading systemic change. The pastors realize that they are not alone. God used this cluster process in GHC to create a team of pastors who no longer compete with each other but who support, help, and encourage one another.

CHAPTER FOUR

Reconnaissance

Strategy Two: The Consultation, Part One

Edward contacted me about conducting a consultation with his congregation. Edward was not only frustrated with what was not occurring under his leadership; he was questioning his outlook on vocational ministry and whether he should remain in his vocation or simply do ministry as an avocation.

God had blessed Edward's ministry in many ways. The congregation had grown during his tenure, the facilities were more than adequate, and the congregation seemed contented since many of their ministry expectations were being met. However, Edward found he no longer enjoyed the task of being a pastor, there had been little growth recently, and he felt his time was consumed with running organizational laps that produced little but boredom.

Edward did an excellent job of preparing the materials required before the actual assessment began on-site. His council and staff members had done their homework, and I had a good feel for the congregation before I ever arrived on the scene. The weekend had been laid out as I had requested and people were on time for interviews and focus groups.

As with any congregation, the materials created in advance (in this case both a congregational survey and a self study), interviews, focus groups, and other conversations revealed the particular strengths and weaknesses that characterized this part of God's church. Edward, his staff members, the members of his council, and other leaders responded with openness to the analysis that I provided, along with the prescriptions of what was required in order to become more effective in accomplishing Jesus Christ's mission for this congregation.

Edward will tell you, though, that the turning point for him and for the congregation occurred in my two-hour interview with him. I looked him in the eye and asked him when he was going to stop being a manager and become a leader. For Edward, that question was profound. It changed his

view of his role. He realized God had called him to function as the leader of the congregation. Today Edward's congregation has doubled in size, the congregation has purchased a large parcel of land for future growth, and a multitude of new disciples have been made.

Edward is so impressed with what the consultation process has done for him, he now assists his judicatory leader in conducting consultations in his part of the country. Edward realizes that God used the consultation process to not only change his congregation but, more importantly, to change him, as he serves his Lord in the church.

Introduction

Congregational consulting was never a ministry I thought about when I was in seminary. In fact for a number years I would have seen myself as the last person a congregation would want to call for assistance, since I did not know what to do to help myself, let alone help others. However, God changed all that and has opened a door of ministry that, while never conducted on a full-time basis, has consumed much of my time and energy for some twenty-five years. Also, working with more than five hundred congregations ranging from twenty-three to three thousand-plus in worship, in at least forty denominational settings, has allowed me to see most of the problems that any congregation can present to a consultant. I am a far more effective consultant today than I was years ago because of what God has taught me through many mentors and the experience of working with so many different parts of Christ's body for so many years.

I have come to learn that leading congregational change, whether as a pastor or a consultant, is ultimately a spiritual battle. True success for a congregational consultant is in proportion to the role the Spirit of God plays in energizing congregations and their leaders to change. This means that all congregational consulting must be undertaken with much prayer before, during, and after the actual consulting process. When we were leading transformation within the region, we usually had a team of people praying the entire weekend during which one or more consultations were taking place.

As usual, God expects us to pray and invoke his work in our behalf and then go and lead the work he has called us to perform. This is especially true for consultants. We must be constantly learning and developing in our efforts to be consultants that really offer congregations help that would not come any other way. Highly effective pastors can benefit from good congregational consultations. Effective pastors and those producing at marginal levels of effectiveness definitely need the help of a good consultant. Most pastors cannot lead systemic change or significant change quickly by themselves.

The major difference between a highly effective pastor and a highly effective consultant is that the pastor knows how to conduct successful ministry one way. However, the consultant has seen successful ministry conducted in a variety of ways and realizes that one way of doing ministry does not work for every pastor or congregation.

Consulting, like much of ministry, is both an art and a science. Many people can learn the science of consulting, including the content of what needs to be shared with congregations at various times in a variety of developmental levels. It is the art of consulting that separates great consulting from good or mediocre consulting.

Finally I recognize that different consultants come at the task of consulting in different ways, with different philosophies and varying perspectives. I will be approaching the consulting task from my experience of what has worked in our region to produce the miraculous turnaround we have experienced. This perspective continues to work as we test it out in various denominational settings across the United States, Canada, New Zealand, and Australia. How our perspective might work in other national and cultural settings I do not know, since we have not employed it in other nations. However, in the nations I have mentioned, the perspective we implement in our consulting process continues to be the key human tool God is using to produce change in the congregations with whom we work.

Congregational Life Cycles Determine Perspective

Congregations, as living organisms, grow up, mature, and die. We often refer to newly born congregations as church plants. We hope that these new plants will mature and develop into full-blown congregations. We also talk of those congregations that cease to exist as having died. In that light we now understand that congregations, like people, have life cycles. Unlike people, however, congregations can have multiple life cycles. Human beings only get one life cycle, and the only way that life cycle can be altered is with resurrection. Since God is not raising most believers from the dead at this point, resurrection is for us a future hope.

The good news is that congregations can have multiple life cycles. There is no guarantee that God will provide a new life cycle for a congregation. In fact, most of the congregations we know about in the New Testament are dead. They may have had multiple life cycles, but at some point God let them die. As we see throughout the history of the church, our God loves to bring life out of death. As often as old congregations die, God brings new ones to life. Yet God at times also brings new life to a congregation by helping that congregation create a new life cycle, stopping the decline that may be present in its current life cycle. In fact, when we speak of "turnaround congregations" or congregations experiencing transformation, we are describing congregations that are beginning new life cycles rather than continuing on in their current one, since to do so would lead to eventual death.

Consulting with congregations that are on the upside of their current life cycle is different from consulting with those on the downward side. It is fair to say that most congregations are on the downward side of their current life cycle, since most congregations in our nation are either in decline or on a plateau. There are crucial differences in how one consults with congregations on the upward versus the downward side of the life cycle.

Congregations that are healthy and growing (indicating they are on the upward side of their current life cycle) still need true consultations. By that I mean the consultant helps the leaders know what is required to become both more effective and efficient in their behaviors in order to move from their current level of effectiveness to the next level of effectiveness. The consultant often provides new information about either what needs to happen or how the systems in place can be improved in order to function better. The consultant may also interact with personnel issues, helping the leaders know either how current leaders should function differently or what new staff members are required and what gifts and skills are needed in order to keep the congregational trajectory moving upward. Finally, the consultant may offer good advice on the current use of facilities or what land and facilities the congregation needs to purchase or build in order to serve well their current congregation while reaching out to new people.

Consulting with congregations on the downside of their current life cycle is a different matter, however, particularly if they have been headed downward for two or more years. At this point the consultation becomes an intervention, since systemic, not incremental, change is required. The longer the congregation has been on this downward trend, the more dysfunctional it becomes in dealing with both group and individual behaviors. And the more dysfunctional it becomes in its behaviors, the harder it is to lead the kind of changes that are required to produce a new life cycle. That is why the term *intervention* is a better one to describe what happens when consulting with such congregations.

Not all consultants are good at every phase of consulting. Just as in other professions (lawyer, doctor, teacher, counselor, and the like), no one is an expert in all the disciplines represented in her or his profession. Success in helping congregations go through transformation when they are on the down side of their current life cycle not only takes special consulting skills, it demands a change of systems that produces new life cycles consistently among a majority of the congregations being consulted. That is what this book is all about. God is using the processes described here to produce consistent systemic change in a majority of the congregations being consulted.

Therefore this book is slanted toward helping those congregations that have been on the down side of their life cycle for some period of time. This is true for most congregations in the United States, regardless of their denominational affiliation. It is even more prevalent in the mainline denominations, although the mainline denominations often have the resources to implement well the strategy being described.

Consultations versus Interventions

Dr. Greg Wiens is a good congregational consultant. He is a great congregational interventionist. He has created a number of important distinctions between that which is a congregational consultation and a congregational intervention. Much of the material I will be presenting in this section I have learned from Greg.

Often in a congregational consultation the consultant is called in to handle issues that are obvious and have often been articulated for the consultant. Some examples might be the need for more room for worship or other key ministries, or staff needs that are obvious because the current staff is overburdened with just maintaining current ministry responsibilities in the face of continual growth. In interventions, however, the key issues most often are not the stated ones. It may be obvious that the congregation is declining rather than growing, or that giving is not keeping up with current budget needs. Usually, however, these are symptoms of much deeper needs, of which many or all the people in the congregation are not even aware. Of course, in any consultation there are some underlying issues that must be addressed. In interventions, though, the underlying issues have already produced significant disability for conducting congregational ministry and, if not addressed, will eventually lead to the congregation's death—or at least its failure to minister in any kind of meaningful way.

Consultations normally handle relatively few issues, since there is already a great deal of health in the congregation. Interventions on the other hand must handle a multiplicity of issues. Transformation in a complex system like a congregation is not simply a matter of amputating one aspect and replacing it with a newer and better part. It requires going back to the foundations and rebuilding. New systems need to be created and then realigned with the new subsystems required to conduct ministry effectively. In one sense a "turnaround" congregation is like starting a new congregation, but using the existing resources such as the congregation, facilities, budget, and so forth.

A consultation may challenge the leaders to stretch and take some risks. Those challenges and risks are usually easier to accept and implement when effective ministry is happening throughout the congregation. The pastor usually has the leverage required to attempt the needed changes since the track record is good and people can more easily see how the changes, if implemented well, will benefit both individuals and the congregation.

In an intervention the consultant often points to a looming crisis, even when things seem to be going well on the surface. The purpose of describing a crisis is to generate urgency. If there is no felt need for change, people will not perform the tough tasks required to create a new life cycle. Therefore, the consultant acts as a catalyst for change by "creating" a crisis. Obviously, this must be done well, and it is just as important for the consultant to offer hope while generating great unrest with the leaders of the congregation.

A consultation usually offers the leaders a series of options in how to pursue the best course of action for improved effectiveness. In fact, good consultants are able to see several ways to address a problem while articulating the advantages and disadvantages of each. An intervention, however, must usually be an all-or-nothing choice. That does not mean that several ways to act are not offered; they are. But despite what will feel to them like great risk, the congregation needs to act soon; inaction can only lead to the death of the congregation. This means that the remedies are prescribed and little choice is offered in how and when they will be implemented.

A consultation often points out where problems occurred originally and how those problems now contribute to the current situation. Often in an intervention the problems have been around and ignored for such a long time that going back to their point of origin is not even helpful. The consultant will take the time to demonstrate that the current problem has its roots in the DNA of the congregation. Still, the focus must be on the current remedy and that which needs to occur soon to provide health before disease and sickness make death the only option.

The consultant often uses questions to guide leaders to the right ideas in a consultation. Usually the leaders individually and collectively possess enough organizational insight and understanding to see what needs to occur if the right questions are asked of them. In an intervention the consultant uses questions to point out great discrepancies and to confront poor behaviors. The consultant also knows that the answers to the questions will not usually lead to insight and appropriate behavior. Instead, the consultant will usually need to be quite direct in identifying the remedies required to reverse the situation.

In a consultation the consultant functions much more as a facilitator, encouraging people to choose the better options. The consultant provides the wisdom that can only come from the experience of seeing ministry done well in a wide variety of settings. Although the consultant is actively involved, the consultant usually functions with greater passivity, encouraging the leaders to learn for themselves the best course of action. In an intervention the consultant is much more active and in some ways even confrontational. Often, those in positions of leadership are incapable of acting well even after they are told how they should behave. Past performances have ingrained behavioral habits that are just too hard to break.

Good consultants always set up some kind of accountability process for implementing that which is decided in the process of consulting. However, in a consultation the process assumes a greater degree of volunteerism than in an intervention. The leaders in a consultation usually understand the need for accountability and desire it because they want to see the ministry become more effective. In an intervention the accountability process is demanded (as much as is possible in a variety of settings), since the level of dysfunction will be manifested in a lack of commitment to being held accountable. One purpose of an intervention is to help leaders stop old habits of behavior and create new ones. Until those new habits take hold, accountability will not occur voluntarily.

Consultation	Intervention
Presenting Issues	Systemic Issues
Few Issues	Multiple Issues
Calculated Risks	Risks of Faith
Options	Go For Broke
Problem-Solution	Life or Death
Consultant-Guide	Consultant-Last Hope
Questions	Directions
Consultant-Facilitator	Consultant-Prophet
Accountability Embraced	Accountability Required

Since most congregations need interventions, the rest of this chapter will assume an intervention. In many ways the consultation process is similar to the intervention, but the intervention usually requires an extra step or two in order to be more directive and to provide accountability. Also, I will be using the term consulting, not intervention, since we call both a congregational consultation. Calling it an intervention does not help in bringing about an intervention.

The Initial Process: Preparing for the Weekend

In the strategy being presented, a congregation commits to a consultation once a pastor commits to be involved in a pastoral grouping or cluster. This is why it is good (though not required) to have the lay leaders in a congregation involved in the initial process of recruiting, if possible. Usually pastors can convince their lay leaders that a consultation is good. If they cannot, that inability communicates volumes about both the pastor and the congregation; neither the pastor nor the congregation should have been selected to be a part of the first group to be used in the strategy.

Once the date is set for the weekend part of the consultation, the pastor is instructed on what is required to prepare the congregation for the weekend. Remember that the consultation is a two-part process: the initial weekend, followed by a one-year process of walking alongside the congregation, coaching it to implement well the prescriptions that are provided during the initial weekend.

When I work with a smaller congregation, I use a congregational self-study (found in the appendix of my book *Direct Hit*). Other consultants may use this tool as well, or others they have developed. Bill Hoyt, who oversees congregational transformation in GHC, uses the self-study and an online survey that he has developed. The point of all these tools is to obtain key information from the congregation about itself before one ever arrives for the weekend. Therefore, the self-study basically asks the congregation to provide a wide variety of data that needs to be collected and collated in order to be sent back to the consultant.

I usually want the self-study document in the hands of the pastor and lay leaders a minimum of two months prior to the weekend. I tell the pastor that his or her role is to have the lay leadership group (board, council, elders, deacons, or the like) assign different people in the congregation the parts of the self-study for which they are to obtain and organize the information being requested. As the material is collected the pastor and lay leadership group are to look at it and learn from that which is being discovered.

There are several reasons for having the pastor and lay leaders look at the material as it is being generated. First, I want the material they are researching and organizing for the self-study to benefit them by providing initial insight into the state of the congregation. Often I have been told by both pastors and lay leaders that this research helped them begin to understand why the congregation was facing the problems they were sensing but had not yet been able to understand. Sometimes they are amazed to realize that the current issues producing organizational stress had surfaced several times in the history of the congregation. One congregation realized that even though they thought they were growing, plotting out their membership numbers on a graph proved that they were stuck on a plateau.

Second, I want the lay leaders to buy into the process before I ever arrive on their campus. The more time and energy they invest in the self-study, the more they are ready to listen when I arrive and usually the more they are open to implementing the prescriptions I will give them.

I ask the leaders of the congregation to send me the self-study document a minimum of three weeks before the weekend consultation. I also ask that, along with the self-study document, they send me all the materials the congregation has in print. This includes items such as budgets, annual reports, church bulletins, brochures and materials given to visitors, job descriptions, minutes from board or council meetings, newsletters, and so forth. The packet of material that is sent to me can be quite large, even for smaller congregations.

Upon receiving the material I begin to read through it and look at all the items that accompany the self-study document. The first thing I am looking for in the self-study document is how it is put together. Is it collected neatly, haphazardly, or messily? Also, I want to see if one person has dominated the organization and presentation of the material, or if the self-study is really the effort of the leaders as a group. I look at not only the material that is included in the document but also at what is not included. Some of what is missing simply reflects poor record-keeping or materials that cannot be found. In other cases, however, the gaps in the material reflect the leaders' desire to keep me from seeing or knowing about certain things. (Since I am not always sure which is which, I will investigate that when I arrive on campus.) I also look at the ways all the other documents are produced. Again, one can easily tell a lot about a congregation just by looking at their materials. For example, many congregations believe that every part of a page should have print on it, while others do not realize there are other colors besides black. On the other hand, some congregations spend lots of money, time, and energy producing well-designed brochures and periodicals that will be distributed to the congregation. Perhaps that may be money well spent, or it may reflect image without substance.

I normally read through the material that has been sent a minimum of three times. The first time is just to get an overview of the entire congregation: its history, demographics, insights into itself, staff and board relationships, and so on. The second time through, I begin to generate questions. The nature of the questions reflects other data I will need to investigate once I am on the campus, strong suspicions I want confirmed or denied, issues I want answered verbally even though I already know what those answers will be, and perceptions or realities I want on the record as people affirm or deny certain things. The purpose of reading the material the third time through is simply to see what observations I have missed up to that point or to generate any other questions that will need to be asked once I am on the campus. If there are any major discrepancies in the material, I will call the pastor or other leaders ahead of time in order to make sure I understand the data or to resolve apparent incongruities.

After completing the questions, I create a tentative list of the congregation's top five strengths, its top five concerns, and the five prescriptions I believe the congregation will need to implement first in order to both start a new life cycle and begin to grow. When this work is done, I feel as though I am ready to visit the congregation and conduct the weekend consultation.

It is important to know that during this entire time of study I have been praying for the congregation, the pastor, the leaders, myself, and the weekend consultation. I clearly understand two spiritual concepts. First, this congregation does not belong to me, nor does it belong to the people who make up the congregation. It belongs to Jesus Christ, who redeemed this part of his church with his blood. He has instituted it to accomplish his mission. He has placed it in this community with certain resources to accomplish that mission. Therefore, I do not want to say or do anything that would interfere with his church accomplishing his mission in this setting. My goal is to enhance this congregation's ability to accomplish that mission.

Second, I understand that if the Spirit of God does not show up that weekend, nothing of eternal consequence will happen. It is surely not by my wisdom or persuasion that any congregation changes for the better from our Lord's perspective. It is only as the Spirit of God works in my life, the pastor's life, the lay leaders' lives, and the lives of individuals in the congregation that anything of spiritual value occurs. Therefore, from the time I initially receive the information until the weekend is complete, I am praying that God will use this event to better align this congregation with God's mission for the church of Jesus Christ.

The Weekend: Interviews

Often the first thing I do upon arriving is to drive through the neighborhoods around the congregation's location and, if possible, see as much of the church building as I can. This provides both a feel for whom God may be calling this congregation to reach and its potential to reach them.

I usually spend the first two hours interviewing the pastor. Before the interview I usually have obtained some good information about the pastor. The self-study always reveals some insight about the pastor. Then the bulk of the information comes from both the judicatory person overseeing the strategy and the cluster mentor. The cluster mentor has had opportunity to interact with this pastor for a number of months and observe that particular pastor's interaction both with the mentor and other pastors. Although I will ask many questions in that two-hour period, I am looking for some crucial pieces of data as I interview:

- Is this pastor capable of leading systemic change with help?
- Does this pastor have the self-awareness to respond well to coaching?
- Does this pastor understand how congregations really function?
- Is this pastor committed to the long haul even in the face of adversity?
- Does this pastor have the political skills to exercise leadership behavior?
- Is this pastor a lifelong learner, and if not is he or she open to becoming one?
- Does the pastor have an accurate understanding of the state of the congregation?
- Does the pastor know what he or she does not know? Is he or she open to help?

- What has the pastor done well?
- What mistakes has the pastor made and what has been the cost of these mistakes?
- How much is the pastor willing to risk personally for the sake of change?
- Does the pastor possess spiritual character and personal integrity?
- Does the pastor's family support him or her, and what is their life situation?

I then spend time interviewing any other ministry or support staff members. In many smaller congregations these people are usually being paid on a part-time basis or are volunteers. I do not spend more than about one-half hour with each person. As I interview I am looking for the following:

- Are they competent to fulfill their current responsibilities?
- Do they understand how their roles fit into the overall congregational ministry?
- What are their perceptions of both the pastoral and lay leaders?
- What do they believe are the congregation's greatest strengths and weaknesses?

After the interviews I then have dinner with the pastor and the pastor's spouse. I ask that this time be reserved just for us and that no other family members or congregational people be invited. Often during that time I ask the spouse questions about the pastor to see how the spouse answers in front of her or his partner. During this interview I am looking for the following:

- How does this couple get along with each other and is there mutual support?
- Is the spouse committed to the ministry in appropriate ways?
- Is the spouse ready for the difficulties that usually accompany systemic change?
- Does the pastor spend appropriate time with his or her family?
- Are there any major unresolved family issues that must be addressed?

The Weekend: Focus Group

In smaller congregations I usually conduct only one focus group. This occurs Friday evening after dinner with the pastor and the pastor's spouse. I ask the pastor to bring together twenty to thirty people who represent a cross section of the congregation. The only people I do not want in this group are lay leaders or the relatives of lay leaders, if that is possible (depending upon the size of the congregation). In every focus group I ask three key questions:

- What do these people believe the strengths of the congregation to be?
- What do these people believe the weaknesses of the congregation to be?
- What are their dreams for the congregation in the next five years?

I am often more interested in how the answers are expressed than in the specific things the group articulates. The answers they give are important, but I want to find out what morale is like and whether or not there is great hope for the future. If there are some people in the group who are relatively new to the congregation, I also ask them how easy or difficult it has been for them to really become part of the congregation.

In some rare cases, where there is a well-defined group in the congregation that is quite frustrated with either the pastor or the direction the congregation is taking, I will meet with them separately. I do this so their responses will not contaminate the main focus group.

The Weekend: Friday Evening

Once the interviews and focus group are completed, I then go back and revise my tentative lists of strengths, concerns, and prescriptions. I find that I usually change two to three things in each list as a result of the work conducted on Friday. Often, something I thought might be quite crucial is not, and another item I had not considered has now become important enough to place on one of the lists. This list is still tentative, since I will spend a good part of Saturday with the leaders of the congregation.

The Weekend: Saturday

I ask the pastor to have the leaders of the congregation meet with me from 9 a.m. to 3 p.m. on Saturday. This includes the pastor and any full-time, part-time, or volunteer staff members. I also invite the official lay leadership group and any other leaders who need to be there. I do not want more than twenty to twenty-five to participate. However, having at least twenty is often good so more leaders can hear and learn. This is a day for some more investigation, as well as training and discussion about what the congregation will need to do in order to create a new life cycle. Lunch is brought in so we can spend a good five hours or so dealing with the key issues I just stated.

I begin by interviewing the lay board, council, elders, deacons, or whatever term is used in that congregation's polity. I do this in front of the others there, so their answers are part of the verbal record of this meeting. One question I do add is that I ask them their expectations for the weekend.

I then spend much of the day describing what healthy and unhealthy congregations look like and how they function. In this training I refer to their congregation often, specifically pointing out where they are healthy or unhealthy. It is in this setting that I often talk about the "elephants in the living room." I address the dysfunction that many smaller congregations need to confront. Through it all, however, I am constantly offering hope of a better tomorrow.

Near the end of our time together (I never go past the stated time), I begin to lay out for the leaders tentative prescriptions that address the issues we have discussed during the day. I want them to hear and have some opportunity to interact with what will probably be in the report that I will give them on Sunday.

The Weekend: The Report

After the group is dismissed I then write the report. The reports are quite brief, never more than four pages, with the usual length being two or three pages. The report consists of the final list of usually five strengths, five weaknesses (which I call concerns), and five prescriptions. In rare instances I may increase the list to six or seven items. For every concern I write a prescription. Each prescription has a deadline indicating the date by which this prescription must be implemented. Most of the deadlines require action within the next six months, in order to give the congregation a sense of momentum as these prescriptions are fulfilled.

One other date is then added to the end of the report. This date is usually four to six weeks from the actual weekend consultation. On this date the congregation will vote to implement or ignore the report (in some polities the vote is to affirm what elders will decide). Regardless of the polity, it is imperative that the congregation vote so the leaders will know the amount of institutional will that exists to make the consultation work. I tell the congregation that the only choices they have are either to accept or reject the report. They do not have the choice to select out of the list of prescriptions the ones they want to accept while rejecting the others. To partially accept the report, or to fail to vote on it at all, is to reject it.

I then tell the congregation that if the report is rejected, then their judicatory is not going to invest in their health and growth anymore. If they accept the report, however, then the judicatory is going to invest in the congregation like they never have in the past. The choice to receive or reject this help is the congregation's.

This is the piece that I find produces the change. If the congregation rejects the report (and about 20 percent of congregations do), then the judicatory no longer has to waste time trying to help them. The congregation has spoken. When the congregation accepts the report, they affirm that they are willing to do the difficult things required to begin to change.

I have learned to put into one or two of the prescriptions what I call "gulp factors." By this I mean prescriptions that, if employed, will cause many in the congregation to "gulp." The willingness to gulp and go on indicates a strong willingness to change. By the way, there is a fine line between a "gulp" factor and a "gag" factor. They will not vote to change if they have to gag.

The Weekend: Sunday

The first thing I do on Sunday is meet with the pastor or the pastor and elders, depending on the congregation's polity. I have e-mailed the report to the pastor (and elders) on Saturday evening after I have completed it. The purpose of this meeting is not to have them change the report but to ask them to help me better express the things I've said, so the congregation can hear them more readily. It is also a courtesy so they are not surprised when I present the report later that day. I then have copies made for everyone in the congregation. These will be distributed as I present the report later.

If there are any personal or family matters that I feel I must discuss with the pastor, I do that in person. I never write anything negative about the pastor in the report. These discussions usually occur on Saturday or on Sunday morning. I also try to enter into such discussions in ways that make them as redemptive as possible for the pastor. I am there to help the pastor be more effective in leading a congregation to health and growth.

I then preach the Sunday morning sermon. The sermon is one of hope that challenges people to risk. I want to establish a biblical basis for a congregation acting in faith. The sermon also sets up the time for giving the report, since in that time I will ask the congregation to act in faith (gulp factors).

After a brief break that may include refreshments or a meal, I give the report to the congregation. This report will take from one hour to an hour and a half to present. I give the congregation a brief overview of what I taught on Saturday. Then I actually read and exegete the report (everyone receives a written copy). My goal is to motivate the congregation to embrace the report. I do this by focusing extensively on hope for a better future.

Following this presentation I tell them what their choices are in regard to the report. On the one hand, they can accept it in its totality and for the next year their judicatory will provide resources to help them implement the report. On the other hand, they can reject the report, in which case the judicatory will focus on other congregations in order to help them become healthy and grow.

I then take questions from the floor. We dismiss on time. I usually stay around to take questions from people who might have been hesitant to ask questions in front of the group. Then the weekend is over.

Summary

The consultation process takes place in two parts. The first part is a consultation weekend. This weekend functions as a line-in-the-sand event for a congregation.

Congregations prepare for the weekend by completing a self-study. This material is sent to the person or persons doing the consulting a minimum of three weeks in advance.

The actual weekend begins with an extended interview with the pastor. Other interviews with key people are conducted, along with a focus group.

An extended time is spent on Saturday with congregational leaders, after which the report is generated. The report usually consists of a list of five strengths, five concerns, and five prescriptions. Each prescription is addressed to one of the concerns and carries with it a deadline for implementation.

Another date is set for four to six weeks following the consultation. This deadline is for the congregation to vote to either accept or reject the report.

The consultant meets with leaders on Sunday to go over the report. The consultant then preaches. Following worship, the consultant presents the report to the congregation. The consultant explains how the report is to be handled in light of the vote in four to six weeks. If they accept the report, the judicatory of which the congregation is a part will assist them by helping them implement prescriptions arising from the consultation. If they reject the report, the judicatory walks away from the congregation, refusing to invest time, money, and energy to help them become healthy and grow.

We have found great results in working with congregations by handling the weekend in this manner. It forces the congregation to make a choice for life or death in cases where the congregation is in the process of dying. It enables us to deal with the dysfunctions while offering great hope. These two forces, honest assessment and hope, are great tools God is using to revitalize congregations.

The second part of the consultation is discussed in chapter 5.

CHAPTER FIVE

Executing the Plan of Battle

Strategy Two: The Consultation, Part Two

The lay leaders of First Church were not denying that the congregation was in trouble. That was clear. What was not clear was how to address the problem. The congregation at one time had reached a total of almost five hundred in worship in two services, and possessed a dynamic children's and youth ministry. However, at the time of the weekend consultation the congregation averaged seventy in one worship service. This loss was made even more dramatic by the fact that the community had grown over 200 percent while this relatively young (less than thirty years old) congregation was in deep decline.

The collective sense of the congregation was that the weekend went well. The major "gulp" factor the leaders faced was embracing a vision of five hundred new disciples coming to Jesus in the next ten years. Also, because the congregation had no place to connect, a "coffee break" was instituted twenty minutes into the morning service to provide a natural way to help the newly created assimilation team network new people and enable those who regularly attended to connect with each other as well as those recently new to the congregation.

Since the congregation embraced the prescription readily, the pastor and lay leaders were provided a congregational coach by the judicatory. The coach was himself an effective pastor, having led a congregation to grow from twenty to over twelve hundred. The coach began to work with the pastor, some key staff members (paid, part-time, and volunteer), and the lay leaders.

The congregation began to grow almost immediately, and some new disciples came into the kingdom of God as a result of the new ways of conducting ministry. There was great excitement as staff members began to achieve the goals for which they were now accountable. The congregational coach met monthly with the pastor, staff members, and lay leaders as needed to help them learn and implement the new systems required for health and growth.

About seven months into the process the pastor and staff attended a Hit the Bullseye conference that targeted congregations that were interested in transforming or in the process of transforming. Part of the conference included visiting former dying congregations that were now changing and making many new disciples regularly and consistently. The staff members were excited about all they saw and encouraged their pastor to lead them to incorporate many of the new ways of functioning when they returned home. However, this event brought a crisis in the life of the pastor, who realized he had taken this congregation as far as he could and was not capable of leading more change. As a result, he resigned his position. This decision left the lay leaders reeling. The congregation was in a process of change, many new changes had already been instituted, and now it looked like all that God had done was going to come to a halt.

Instead, the congregational coach and the judicatory leader walked these leaders through a process of dealing well with the crisis and finding a new pastor who would pick up where the former had left off. Today that congregation is continuing to grow and thrive. That would not have been possible if there had not been a competent coach already in place, and a judicatory leader committed to this strategy who deferred to the coach when necessary. This on-going relationship turned a crisis into a great opportunity for future growth in this healthy, thriving congregation.

Introduction

The consultation (which is an intervention in congregations on a plateau or in decline) is the best human tool I know of that God is using to produce systemic transformation in congregations on a plateau or in decline. It begins with the "line-in-the-sand" weekend, where the congregation is forced to make a choice to live or die. If the congregation chooses to live by accepting the consultation report, then the second part of the consultation begins. The second phase lasts for a minimum of one year. During this year the judicatory assigns to the congregation a congregational coach who commits to walking alongside the congregation. The role of this coach is to make sure the congregation implements the prescriptions in the consultation report, provide training when it is required, bring resources to the congregation to help it succeed, and hold the pastor, staff members, lay leaders, and congregation accountable to implement that which they have agreed to do.

The two parts of the consultation as described are crucial. Both must be handled as described in this book, particularly when the congregation is on the downside of the life cycle. Even when the congregation is on the upside of the life cycle, the weekend is crucial and so too is continuing coaching. But the manner described in forcing choices and promising help or no help depending on the choices made is not mandatory. Congregations on the upside are, one hopes, looking to become more effective in their behaviors in what is already a healthy situation. However, to bring systemic change consistently to unhealthy and dysfunctional congregations, the human tool being described in this book (the weekend consultation/intervention) must be implemented in the manner prescribed.

This is not to say that congregations on the downside of their life cycles cannot be helped in other ways. It is to say that the tools being shared in this book, when employed as stated, produce systemic change more often and with a higher degree of success than any others of which I am aware. God has demonstrated this response through the use of these tools in our region and is now doing so with a number of denominational groups in several different nations.

The Judicatory

In much of the book up to this point I have been talking about what happens with pastors and congregations. Obviously, that must be the focus, along with lay leaders, since denominations are only changed one congregation at a time. However, now I want to go behind the scenes to the part played by the judicatory or association of congregations. I wish to discuss what these entities need to do as the two-part consultation process is happening, integrated with the cluster meetings of pastors.

By the end of the second pastoral cluster meeting, dates should be set for the weekend consultations the pastors will lead their congregations to conduct. The judicatory now knows not only the weekends but, following each weekend (assuming the congregations vote to affirm the consultation report), the timeline for walking alongside each congregation for a minimum of twelve months. An implication of setting these dates means that those congregations that have the weekend part of the consultation scheduled within eight months after the first cluster meeting can then expect judicatory help for at least twelve months after the weekend event occurs.

Since most judicatories find this strategy works so well, and since the pastors usually want the cluster to continue, the strategy then becomes a regular part of judicatory life. In GHC our clusters continue to the present. We still conduct congregational consultations where we work with a congregation for a weekend and then continue to work with them to implement change and produce accountability. The purpose of talking about starting things for a year is to help judicatories and associations see this as an experiment. Even then, I encourage them to try this strategy as a three-year experiment.

Setting the dates for the weekends establishes the timelines for the yearlong portion of the consultation. Once this is in place, the judicatory leader needs to begin to recruit consultants and coaches. If the judicatory does not have anyone competent to conduct these consultations, it means going outside the judicatory to find the right people. (This is one reason I and others have been conducting training for judicatories. GHC now has both formal and on-the-job training for judicatory personnel who need to become equipped to conduct the ministries being described in this book). As stated before, the bottom line criterion for either consultants or congregational coaches is that they have led effective, healthy, growing congregations in situations larger than the congregations they are working with in this process. These people need to perform their tasks from both an intellectual background (they know and understand the disciplines related to change and healthy congregations) and an experiential background (they have done it themselves, not just observed or read about it). This criterion is why most denominations often do not have an adequate number of personnel initially and require training for those who will eventually sustain this strategy long term in their particular denomination.

Once the dates and timelines are established and the consultants and coaches are recruited, the judicatory person needs to begin to network with the congregations that will be experiencing the consultations. The judicatory person's role is to help them see the benefits of what is coming and let them know in advance that the purpose for all of this effort is to help them succeed in the mission God has called the congregation to follow. This person needs to let the congregation know that the judicatory believes in what is happening, is behind what is happening, and will do all in its power to help this congregation become effective again. This person also needs to inform the congregation that what will be required will be difficult, but well worth the effort. The congregation also needs to understand that it will have the opportunity to benefit from many resources not now being offered to many other congregations in the denomination. The congregation should understand, however, that they need to fulfill their responsibilities (the prescriptions arising out of the weekend) in order for the judicatory to continue to stand with them. Finally, the congregation should be informed again that this is not just another transitory program but rather a strategy by which the judicatory can transform itself one congregation at a time—starting with this one.

The judicatory should also be networking with the pastors involved to make sure they are preparing the congregation and the lay leaders well for both the weekend part of the consultation and the year of coaching. Many pastors have little or no idea of how to set these events up to succeed before they ever happen. Often, pastors have never informed even their leaders about what will be happening and how it will happen. Such pastors obviously need to increase their leadership behavior skills. That coaching should begin with the judicatory or associational leader who helps them prepare the congregation for the consulting events. The judicatory leader may want to set up two or three advance meetings with the pastor, lay leaders, and even the congregation to prepare all of them for what will be coming. The more the sense of anticipation can be heightened, the better. In these gatherings the judicatory leader needs to describe what will occur during the weekend, emphasizing the expected benefits as the congregation once again becomes healthy and begins to grow. Hope is a great motivation for performing difficult tasks. The judicatory person also needs to be in contact with the consultant. The purpose of such networking is to inform the consultant about the congregation and the pastor's needs, expectations, fears, and hopes.

The initial consultation should involve a team of people. Comprising the team are the consultant and those the consultant is training to become consultants themselves. The majority of trainees on these teams should be effective pastors who are leading healthy congregations. The role of those being trained is to learn the process, while also providing insight and assistance to the consultant.

One denominational group that had few if any consultants when they first implemented the strategy created and designed a process for training future consultants. I was invited to come in and do some initial consultations and train future consultants during the weekend. Then those on the team who had good pastoral experience and demonstrated an aptitude for consulting conducted more consultations, with new people constantly being added to the team. Then criteria were established to become a congregational consultant. A person had to observe two consultations, help lead two consultations as assistants to a consultant, and then lead two while being observed by a good consultant. This process has resulted in a whole cadre of consultants being trained who are part of that denomination. That means when these individuals show up to conduct the consultation, they are a part of the denomination in which the congregation exists. This takes away any excuse that may come at some consultant who is not part of that congregation's particular denomination.

One key member of the consulting team should be the congregational coach who will walk alongside the congregation for one year. Often the best coaches are current pastors within the denomination who are leading effective, healthy, growing congregations that are making new disciples for Jesus Christ. (If such people become the coaches, it means they can coach no more than one or two congregations for a twelve-month period, since they are busy leading their own congregation.) If this person is part of the weekend team, this individual has experienced firsthand the process and knows the congregation and its pastor and lay leaders very well. This person also knows what has been discussed about change and how those changes need to occur, even though much of what has been said is not in the report. The weekend also helps this person develop a relationship with the pastor, the lay leaders, and in some cases the congregation.

There is one advantage I have in conducting these weekends for judicatories and associations from other denominations. I can constantly let everyone know that I have been employed by that group of congregations to help this one congregation, because the judicatory really wants to see this congregation once again become effective in its mission. I can promote the judicatory leader, the coach that will work with them, and say much about them they usually find difficult to say about themselves. When I give the report to the congregation on Sunday, I make sure they know that this weekend is a gift to them from their judicatory. I lift up their judicatory and the judicatory leader and praise them for their willingness to invest in this particular congregation. I also let the congregation know that the judicatory believes so much in them that they have asked them to be part of this first wave of congregations to experience change.

Specific Judicatory Responsibilities

The first responsibility is related to what happens at the end of the first half of the consultation. When the report is over and the congregation has learned it has four to six weeks to decide to accept or reject the report, the judicatory needs to be ready to tell the congregation that there will be one or two town meetings led by the judicatory staff member, working with the cluster of which the congregation's pastor is a part. In these meetings, the purpose of which is to discuss the report, the judicatory staff member can assist the pastor.

When the meetings are conducted, the congregation needs to see that the judicatory person and the pastor are a team, both wanting the congregation to choose wisely and accept the report. The judicatory person needs to respond honestly and openly to questions, observations, and even critiques. Yet, while responding, the leader needs to encourage the congregation to vote to accept the report. Often the recommendation of the report is presented as a three-year experiment. If it does not work the congregation can go back to its old ways of functioning. Since the current ways of functioning are not working, however, why not try a new way for a while and see if it makes a difference?

The judicatory person needs to do all he or she can to help the congregation as an entity and individuals within it embrace the report. The time between the giving of the report and the decision on the report is a crucial one for both the pastor and the judicatory leader. Both need to be quite active in doing all they can to prepare the way for a positive vote. The weekend consultation has provided momentum for the congregation; the role of the pastor and the judicatory person is to keep that momentum going in a positive direction.

There is a second set of responsibilities the judicatory person needs to embrace. Those responsibilities are related to the prescriptions that are generated in the consultant's report. Usually, one or two of the prescriptions need to be led or facilitated by the judicatory person for two reasons: to reaffirm the judicatory's commitment to the process, and to set the judicatory up to be positively involved in the transformation process.

One example may relate to a common first prescription. That prescription usually involves a day of prayer and fasting for the congregation and its leaders, including the pastor. Such a day requires the help of an outsider to lead the events, since the pastor is involved in that day's requirements as the leader of the congregation. This task is ideal for the judicatory leader. Leading the congregation on this day in this role sets that person up to oversee a very special day of spiritual events that are often the initiation of the coming transformation.

Another example relates to the creation and development of vision. The judicatory leader may be the on-site person helping the pastor and congregation begin the process of dreaming or creating and developing a new vision for the congregation. Again, such a role sets the judicatory person up to be highly visible and involved in a very positive activity designed to help the congregation.

Finally, the judicatory person must be involved with the pastor, lay leaders, or even the congregation throughout that first year, reminding them of the commitments that were made when they voted to embrace the consultation report. There will be times when individuals and groups within the congregation will revert to former habits of behavior. Someone needs to gently and firmly remind them that new habits of behavior are now in force as a result of decisions and commitments made at the conclusion of the consultation weekend.

Although the judicatory leader may not have the effective ministerial experience of the consultant or the congregational coach, they still have a key role to fulfill. In fact, wise judicatory people put themselves at the disposal of the consultant and the congregational coach to do whatever they can to help. To many long-time denominational people, these individuals carry denominational authority. The judicatory people need to be willing to use that authority to help long-time members who are struggling with the change to be open to such change. The less effective congregational experience any judicatory person has, the more that person needs to be dependent upon the consultant and congregational coach to do whatever the experts ask.

It is also my experience that people who do not like the changes may call or e-mail the judicatory office, hoping to find there a sympathetic ear with which to share their complaints. Judicatory office personnel need to know that if they communicate in any way with people making such complaints, they are to affirm what the consultant and others are doing, and let that person know that the judicatory office stands behind what is happening. If this is not done, it undercuts and in some cases curtails all the efforts that have been made up to this point in the life of the congregation. It can sabotage the entire process.

The Actual Coaching

The first thing the congregational coach does upon being appointed (if they were not part of the consultation team) is to read through the consultation report and interact with the person who conducted the consultation and the judicatory person responsible for putting all this together for this particular congregation. The purpose of this meeting is not only to bring the coach up to speed on where the congregation is and what it needs to do but to develop a plan for working with both the pastor and the congregation for the next twelve months. Priorities need to be established for what will happen during the next twelve months, and for the hoped-for results. Also, any private conversations the weekend consultant has had with the pastor about any inadequacies or deficiencies need to be discussed in order that the congregational coach may address them and make sure they are being dealt with by the pastor's personal coach.

The prescriptions often require the pastor to have a personal coach, who is usually a different individual from the congregational coach. It would also be good at this time for the congregational coach to interact with the pastor's personal coach, since it is often recommended that the pastor obtain one. (By the way, if the pastor already has a personal coach and that coach has no effective experience in growing a healthy congregation, the pastor needs to either get a second personal coach or replace the current coach with one who has such experience.) These two coaches, the pastor's personal coach and the congregational coach, need to be working together in order to ensure maximum benefit for both the pastor and the congregation.

Once these strategy sessions have taken place, it is time for the congregational coach to interact with the pastor. (It is assumed the pastor either knows this person, or has been told about this individual and is anxious to work with him or her.) This initial meeting should accomplish three things. First, the coach will lay out with and for the pastor the plan for the year. The priorities that have been agreed upon will be established with the pastor, and strategies and tactics for implementing these priorities will be discussed. Second, dates will be established for when the coach will be on the congregation's campus for the next twelve months. It is imperative that the coach actually show up and interact with the pastor and key lay leaders. The coach appearing on the congregation's campus each month produces an accountability that cannot be achieved in any other format. Third, the pastor and coach work out appropriate protocols for staying in touch between the monthly visits. Many congregational coaches are busy pastors themselves and therefore these coaches must determine how and when the pastor is to contact them, either for follow-up questions or emergencies that might arise.

How the Coach Coaches

The congregational coach is asked to implement a number of tasks. At the top of the list is helping the pastor (who often lacks the coach's leadership skills) develop better leadership behaviors. Most pastors do not know how to produce health and growth. The coach is to help them learn both that which needs to happen and to coach them in how to make it happen.

This means that each month the coach should spend some time with the pastor. This time together has a number of purposes. First, the coach needs to see how the pastor is doing both spiritually and emotionally. Second, the coach needs to learn what the pastor has or has not accomplished since the coach's last visit. It is also important to learn both how things have been accomplished and why certain things have not been done. At the end of the initial weekend consultation, I sometimes have told pastors to do nothing without consulting their coach first. I have done so when I feared the pastor would not know what to do, or that her or she would do the right thing but in the wrong way. The coach also needs to interact with lay leaders or staff on the pastor's behalf. One problem most pastors have is an inability to handle problems well. Sometimes they are too direct in their manner and at other times not direct enough. The coach then needs to make sure that the coach's agenda for being there this particular month is still part of the plan. Finally, the coach needs to lay out what should be accomplished before the coach returns the following month.

A second reason for the coach being on campus each month is to provide training in order to implement the prescriptions coming out of the weekend consultation. In some cases the coach will conduct the training. In other situations the coach might bring in trainers and watch as those people do the training. For example, often the weekend consultation has resulted in a new structure for the congregation. The pastor may now have a number of staff members (people who are clear about their responsibility, have adequate authority to carry out their responsibility, and are being held accountable for their area of responsibility). Some pastors have no idea how to conduct staff meetings and hold staff accountable for their goals. Therefore the coach may actually lead a staff meeting and then discuss with the pastor what was accomplished and how it was accomplished. In another case the coach might bring the coach's children's staff person from the coach's congregation to train the people leading children's ministries in this congregation. The bottom line is that the coach is there to make sure that the training required to meet the prescriptions of the weekend consultation actually happens.

A third reason for the coach to be on the congregation's campus each month is to help the pastor and congregation learn new habits of behavior and unlearn old habits (how they acted in the past). The weekend consultation usually leads a congregation to establish a new lay governance team. Even if the governance team is not new, the people on it often are. In any case this group needs to function differently than it has in the past. This group is now in place to govern, not lead or manage the congregation. The basic task of governance is to hold the leader—the pastor—accountable for goals. The pastor leads, the pastor's staff manages, and the congregation does the ministry.

Often, the coach needs to meet with the governance group initially and then again in three or four months to both train the group in how it is to act and then remind them again to behave in a manner consistent with the initial training. Some of the people in this group likely will revert to former ways of acting and will need to be reminded that such behavior is no longer acceptable in the new way of functioning. These problems will arise in a number of ways, and each time they do, the coach needs to address them. He or she makes sure that the new habits are constantly reinforced by training the pastor to ascertain that such will happen or by personal intervention as the coach.

A fourth reason for being on campus each month is to help deal with the resistance that will surely come to all the new changes. Many people are open to change until the changes affect their favorite ministry or their favorite person who no longer has a place of influence. When this happens, some individuals begin to attack the pastor and others leading the change. These people often bring up things that have yet to go well or have not been handled as well as they might have been. (Incidentally, this problem is the norm in many unhealthy congregations whose pastors lack strong leadership abilities. These congregations did not get this way overnight, nor will they change overnight.) These people leverage these problems as illustrations that the change is not working (which is often not true), and then make a case for going back to the old way of functioning. When this happens, most pastors do not know what to do or how to handle the conflict.

At this point the coach needs to step in (sometimes even between the scheduled monthly meetings) and deal with those leading this outcry. The congregation needs to see that former ways of handling conflict will not be tolerated. Often when I was coaching our congregations in GHC, I would say to the pastor, "Let me come to your board meeting tonight." I would then tell the pastor to share with me what needed to be said, which, had the pastor said it, would have gotten him or her fired. Then we would go to the meeting, where I would say those things by looking people in the eye and telling them that such behavior was wrong and not appropriate. In cases like this, often the judicatory person needs to show up with the coach and add the weight of the judicatory to what is being done. People need to see that conflict is being handled in a new and different manner.

Finally, the coach should be asked to come in and preach once or twice during the twelve months of the coach's involvement with the congregation. This will give the coach opportunities to lift up the new mission and vision and to commend the pastor and new lay leaders for all they are doing to lead change.

Good coaching takes a lot of hard work on the part of both the coach and the leaders being coached. That is why experience is so important in the coach. Coaching cannot be done from theory but from the coach's experience as an effective pastor in leading (currently or in the past) a healthy, growing, effective congregation. Such coaching allows effective pastors to have a Kingdom impact beyond their own congregation. It gives them the opportunity over a number of years to influence many congregations and pastors. In areas where the coach is geographically close to the congregations being coached, such coaches are then able to help implement a strategy to change their city, county, or towns for Jesus Christ.

Also, pastors learn best when they are in some kind of an apprenticeship. Thus, when they have a personal coach with effective congregational experience, a congregational coach with effective congregational experience, and a judicatory leader who is helping them deal with fundamental issues of behavior and content, they usually succeed as pastors. This is where pastoral leadership for those without the gift and talent is developed. It can't happen in a classroom. Instead it happens in the crucible of ministry in accountable relationships, with those who are further along in their learning and who are experienced in guiding, teaching, and coaching. It is this process that has and is helping many ineffective pastors become effective at what God has called them to do: lead healthy, growing congregations.

Summary

All congregational consultations are in two parts. Congregations on the downside of their life cycle need a consultation that functions like an intervention. Such interventions have two aspects or parts. The first part is a weekend "line-in-the-sand" event. In this event the congregation hears what it must do within certain time frames. If they accept this prescription and embrace it, the second part takes over. The second part is the commitment by the judicatory to walk alongside the congregation for the next twelve months.

The judicatory has already been working behind the scenes to make all of this happen. They have been organizing pastors into monthly cluster meetings led by mentors who have more effective congregational experience than anyone in the cluster. The judicatory has also been finding and training consultants to do the consultations. It has also been recruiting the coaches who will walk alongside the congregations for twelve months in order to help the congregation implement the prescriptions coming out of the weekend consultation report.

Once the congregation embraces the weekend report the judica-tory appoints a congregational coach to help the congregation for twelve months. This coach has effective experience in leading a congregation to health and growth. This coach commits to being on the congregation's campus each month.

The coach meets each month with the pastor to determine what has been occurring in relation to the consultation report. The coach conducts training or brings to the congregation the training people need to be effective in their new roles. The coach also helps the congregation create new habits of behavior while stopping old habits of conduct. The coach confronts or helps the pastor confront those who at any time during the year try to stop the changes by creating conflict. Finally, the coach comes on the weekend several times to be the cheerleader for the new change and the work that the pastor and lay leaders are doing to lead the change.

CHAPTER SIX
Recruiting the Soldiers

Strategy Three: Training the Laity

The congregation had once been strong. As a new church plant it had grown rapidly, with hundreds in worship. But those days were long gone, even though the congregation was less than a decade old. Now fifty to sixty adults in worship was a good Sunday. What made the situation even worse was that while attendance had been declining, the neighborhood had been growing by leaps and bounds. The once large fish in a small neighborhood pond was now the little fish that had been swallowed up by a huge neighborhood that simply ignored the nice little church on the corner.

The pastor had been recruited by his associational leader to be part of a monthly cluster designed to help pastors learn how to bring congregational health to their congregations while also learning how to become leaders and not function simply as chaplains. When the pastors were told that two lay training events were part of the overall strategy for change, this young pastor volunteered to hold the event on his congregation's campus. He also made the commitment to have the congregation handle all the logistics and provide all the refreshments as a gift to the other congregations represented in the cluster. As a result, this pastor's congregation had an excellent turnout for the training event. All their board members were there, along with many other key leaders in the congregation. This congregation probably had more representation per capita than any other congregation that attended.

The host congregation for the lay training event had scheduled their weekend consultation for two weeks after the lay training event was held on the campus. During the Saturday training with the board and other lay leaders, the consultant found them open to the required changes. When he asked why, the congregational leaders replied that what they had learned at the lay training event made sense and they wanted to start as quickly as possible to regain health, begin to grow, and see God use this congregation to once again impact the community that now surrounded the church. Lay staff members shared how they were already

dreaming of doing ministry differently in order to reach children and young people.

On Sunday, as the consultant shared the report with the congregation and detailed the prescriptions, including a number of "gulp" factors, he found little resistance. Instead the questions that came were more about how to implement the prescriptions than whether to accept them.

The consultant realized that having a majority of the congregation at the lay training event had prepared them to embrace the change process and made them eager to implement the prescriptions. In some cases the congregation was ready to move faster than the pastor and staff members. The lay training event had provided hope and given the people an understanding of both the what and the whys required for change. As a result, they were ready to trust God and move ahead.

Introduction

The process of leading transformation with the majority of congregations requires that we develop a strategy that includes the pastor (and the pastor's family), the congregation, and the judicatory (or some other outside help). The strategy being described in this book works because it does include all these elements. The pastors are involved in monthly cluster meetings with mentors who have themselves been effective in leading congregational transformation. The pastor and lay leaders have been confronted directly in the consultation process by consultants and coaches who also know from experience what congregational transformation requires. The congregation is addressed when the report of the weekend consultation is presented. The congregation is also affected by decisions made throughout the year as the report is implemented. And, of course, the judicatory or association of congregations has been intimately involved in organizing, funding, and implementing the strategy.

The process thus far is good as far as it goes. An important piece of the puzzle is still missing, however. The congregation as a group of disciples has not received any training about congregational health and growth. The individuals in the congregation need this training for their development as disciples. It is also important to conduct this training in order for the strategy to be implemented well and with success. I have found that when the laity "get it" there is an eagerness to move forward, even at the expense of losing those few people who do not want the change to take place.

Therefore, the third piece of the strategy is to conduct two lay training events within twelve months. The pastors in the cluster are expected to do all they can to get as many as possible in their congregations to attend these two events. The more people who attend, the easier the change process will be and the faster it will go. It is important for the silent majority in congregations to learn about the urgency most congregations are facing, while being confronted with the foolish behaviors of how this urgency is not being addressed. These people also need to hear how the process can bring new wisdom, and with it new hope, to the system. When this happens, many individuals want change for their setting, particularly when they learn how other congregations just like theirs are making such changes.

Not every congregation will respond in a positive manner, but in my experience the majority do, and these two events produce great motivation to either have the consultation soon or to move forward with the prescriptions they received during their recent consultation.

The two lay events usually are conducted on a Friday evening and Saturday morning schedule or in an extended Saturday session that runs from 9 a.m. to 3 p.m. Some judicatories only schedule the event for three hours on a Saturday. When less time is provided for such training, however, the results are usually in proportion to the energy invested.

When I conduct these two events I focus on two specific areas. I begin by talking about congregational health and disease. Most of my time is spent showing congregations what it takes to actually become healthy. I cover the same material that I talk to pastors about in the cluster meeting and that I use with lay leaders on the Saturday during the weekend consultation. That is why this strategy is called a layered learning strategy: I keep coming back to the same basic material time after time with everyone.

During the second lay training event I show how to make the Great Commission the foundational value that drives all congregational behavior. I believe each congregation has the same mission: to regularly and consistently make new disciples for Jesus Christ. Therefore if each congregation is to be making new disciples, the Great Commission must be the foundational value that drives everything a congregation does. It also means that the vision and all behaviors of the congregation must be evaluated in relation to how well the Great Commission is being implemented in the life of the congregation.

The rest of this chapter will be an overview of what I teach when I conduct these two training events. Therefore it is important that I share these next few thoughts about the source of my teaching. All of us are indebted to those great saints who preceded us, and on whose shoulders we stand. We are also the product of many teachers, some of whom have taught us formally in the classroom, while others have done it through their writing, speaking, or friendships. Then there are those who have functioned as mentors. Again, in some cases this may have been done formally or informally.

I will always be indebted to Haddon Robinson, who was not only my homiletics professor but also mentored me as I taught homiletics alongside him in a seminary context. The three people who have influenced me the most, though, in developing the content of these lay events are Leith Anderson, George Bullard, and Frank Tillapaugh. Leith and Frank are two people with whom I had the privilege to work. George has been a person I have learned from at several key times in my life. I just hope they forgive me for any license I have taken with their material and for rearranging it in order to make it my own. I am also indebted to my wife, Teresa, who keeps reminding me to teach in such a way that pastors and their families are constantly learning how to deal with the stresses often brought about by congregational transformation. Her deep concern for ministerial families led her to write her book *Women Married to Men in Ministry: Breaking the Sound Barrier Together*.

Congregational Health and Growth

Three Assumptions
I always begin with three basic assumptions that are foundational to teaching and communicating about change. The first comes from

creation: everything that is healthy grows. That is why we closely monitor our newborn children to see if they are putting on weight and growing in inches. Babies that fail to put on weight and grow in length are seriously ill. Growth does not prove health, but the lack of growth clearly proves unhealthiness. Therefore, if the church of Jesus Christ is a living, growing organism, God expects growth. The assumption thus is that congregations that are not growing are sick. Clearly there is more disease in the body than there is health.

The second assumption comes from the Bible. Jesus Christ said that he would build his church and the gates of hell would not prevail against it. Therefore the purpose of the church is basically to make sure that the Evil One, who because of sin and evil holds most of the world hostage, does not win. The church of Jesus Christ was designed to depopulate the Evil One's zip code by constantly making new disciples. Congregations failing to accomplish this mission are living in disobedience to the Lord of the church. The assumption therefore is that congregations failing to regularly and consistently make new disciples for Jesus Christ are living in disobedience to their Lord.

The third assumption relates to culture. While the gospel of Jesus Christ has not changed, the church of Jesus Christ has been changing constantly in order to take the unchangeable message to a constantly changing culture. The assumption is that small congregations of two hundred or less in worship (which is the large majority of all congregations in our nation) are small because they are designed to be small. Large congregations (more than two hundred in worship) are larger because they are designed to be large. We have learned that the only way small congregations can become larger is to act like large congregations while they are small. In other words they must act the size they want to become.

Congregational Life Cycles

I stated in my two other books (*Hit the Bullseye* and *Direct Hit*) that as we began to work with congregations, we introduced them to the concept of congregational life cycles. We told them that one way of assessing congregational health was to determine where they were as a congregation in relation to their current life cycle.

Obviously, since most congregations are on the downward side of their current life cycle, we need to help them know how to create a new one in order to again be healthy and grow. In essence the first lay training event helps congregations know what it takes to create a new life cycle and how to make it happen in their particular congregation.

The day of training involves looking at four key concepts that, if aligned correctly, enable a congregation to move from being on the downward side of their current life cycle to starting a new one, which in turn puts them on the upward side. Those key concepts are vision, relationships, ministries, and structure (VRMS).

In the vision section we discuss the mission of the congregation and then vision itself.

In the relationship section we deal with five ideas:

- Connecting people with people in order to make friends;
- Creating third places so people can be accepted for who they are;
- Learning the purpose of different size groups;
- Understanding the difference between change and transition;
- Finding your niche as a congregation.

In the ministries section we teach how to become a staff-led congregation, which includes the setting of key goals.

In the structure section we lay out the Accountable Model of Leadership:

- The Board (Session, Council, Deacons) *governs* the church;
- The Pastor *leads* the church;
- The Pastor's Staff *manages* the church;
- The Congregation *conducts* the ministries of the church.

Mission and Vision

I always start with mission or purpose. I want the lay leaders to understand that every congregation has a mission. The major question is whether the leaders are conducting a mission that suits the agenda of the people attending (meaning it is inward) or whether the congregation has joined Jesus Christ in his mission for his church, which is to make new disciples regularly and consistently (making it outward). I find this teaching is the key to congregational transformation. Systemic change is required to move a downward life cycle to a new life cycle, moving upward. Once a congregation makes a decision to move outward, we then tell them that every ministry in the congregation must demonstrate how they are actually helping make new disciples.

Although the mission issue is the most crucial change a congregation on the downside of a life cycle must make, the most difficult thing for a majority of pastors and congregations to figure out is the vision piece. Therefore, when working with a congregation, I help them develop their first vision by using a rather simple format.

This format assumes that the vision is a description of what their community (not their congregation) will look like if the mission is actually implemented. Second, if the mission is about making new disciples for Jesus Christ, the vision must also be about the making of new disciples. Finally, the vision (or the first major segment connected to the vision) must have a number in it. The purpose of this number is to produce accountability throughout the life of the congregation.

I ask a congregation to describe its community geographically. This is the community the congregation believes God is calling it to reach. It may be a town, county, section of a city, or so forth. I then ask the leaders to tell me the number of people in their community who do not attend any congregation on a regular basis. (I do not ask them to look at denominational affiliation, since if people do not go to church, their denominational affiliation is probably irrelevant— plus God calls us to make disciples, not denominational adherents.) I then challenge the congregation to determine the percentage of those people who do not attend church that God will help them lead to become disciples in the next five years. I challenge congregations to make reaching 1 percent, 4 percent, 7 percent, or even 10 percent of the unchurched in their community their vision.

One major advantage to looking at vision this way is to point out that the vision does not speak to the size the congregation will become in the next five years, but rather the impact the congregation will have on its community as it seeks to do its mission. I have found that coming at vision like this energizes a congregation, since the focus is truly on others, not themselves. Such a vision gives the congregation a target, a time frame in which to trust God for big things, and the freedom to then develop strategies to achieve this goal. It ties the vision directly to the mission and then produces rigorous accountability.

Relationships

The first thing I help congregations understand is that people new to the congregation are not looking for a friendly church but for friends. In many smaller congregations making friends is most difficult. First, it must happen with intentionality and this concept is not one the people in smaller congregations understand. Second, members of smaller congregations have all the friends they can currently handle. Therefore we teach the congregation that someone in their group must be willing to forego connecting with their friends for a while in order to start connecting with new people. Then, as the congregation increases its visitor flow, the person responsible for connecting with others moves from being a friend to newer people to networking the newer individuals with each other so they can make friends among themselves.

We then discuss how people are looking for not only friends but a place where they can be accepted for who they are, not what they do. One major reason for small groups is to help people find other individuals with whom they can find significance and acceptance. We show these congregations what they need to do to create new cells within the body, so that as these cells multiply, the body of people within the congregation grows.

I find that in dealing with different size groups within the congregation, I spend more time helping them understand the purpose of large-size groups and the role this plays in Sunday worship. Many smaller congregations run their Sunday morning much more for fellowship and connecting than they do to advance a mission and vision. This happens because in many of these congregations, fellowship and connecting are not happening anywhere else during the week.

We then talk about the difference between change and transition. I point out that change always starts with a new beginning and comes to me from the outside. However, transition always begins with a loss and it is what affects me on the inside. All good changes produce losses for some people. Therefore, we show how to have both a plan for change and a plan for dealing with the transitions that accompany the changes.

Finally, we discuss how each congregation has a niche in the community. I believe that God gives each part of the body (a congregation) the gifts and talents that are required to reach certain people in the community God has called it to reach. Therefore, we want congregations to know their community and then evaluate how God has designed their congregation to best reach the segment of the community God calls them to serve.

Ministries

I spend a great deal of time talking about ministries, since this is where we help congregations (especially smaller ones) understand what it means to become a staff-led congregation. I tell them that the word "staff member" has nothing to do with whether a person is paid or not paid. Rather, this term reflects the marriage of responsibility, authority, and accountability. Volunteers can be staff members, as well as others who are paid to lead ministries.

We then discuss how missional congregations accomplish their mission by staffing for those ministries people expect when they come into a church. Missional congregations start where people are to move them to where they should be. The overall strategy is to convert consumers into fully devoted disciples of Jesus Christ. Many congregations start with people where people in the congregations expect them to be, not with where the people really are in their spiritual pilgrimage.

Each congregation has two constituencies: those within the congregation who need to be ministered to and those outside the congregation who need to become disciples of Jesus Christ. Ministries designed for those already in the congregation exist to help mobilize them to reach the constituency outside the church's walls, for which the congregation as a whole exists.

Congregations are taught to place staff members over those ministries that all congregations are expected to have in this culture. Congregations then give these staff members the authority to conduct these ministries any way they see fit, with the understanding that such staff members will be held accountable for measurable goals once a year. Staff members who achieve their goals are allowed to remain in charge of their respective areas of ministries. Staff members who do not achieve their goals are then asked to step down from leading their areas of ministries. We teach congregations that you can hold individuals accountable, which you cannot do with committees.

All staff members must set the same three goals, along with all other goals that relate to each area of ministry for which individual staff members have oversight. The first goal is the number of new disciples that will come to Jesus through that particular area of ministry. The second goal is the number of new leaders that each staff member will develop. And the third goal is the percentage by which that particular area of ministry will grow during the year. The totals of all these goals then become the pastor's goals for the year, since the staff members work for the pastor.

The two biggest human dynamics in turning around congregations are getting them to function outward with an exciting vision and then teaching them to act like a large congregation. All congregations, regardless of size, must act like they are functioning with hundreds or thousands of people in attendance.

Structure

We cover three major issues in dealing with structure. The first issue is that the leader (the pastor) must be growing and developing as a leader while developing other people to be leaders within the congregation. Congregations grow as two specific areas are multiplied: groups and leaders. All of this assumes the pastor sees functioning as a leader (not a chaplain) as her or his primary role. Chaplain ministries are to be handled throughout the congregation by believers God has gifted to function in such ways.

The second major issue is that responsibility, authority, and accountability must be married. The board, session, council, or deacons employ the pastor to be the leader and give the pastor both the responsibility and the authority to carry out the congregation's mission and vision. However, this group then holds the pastor accountable for how well that responsibility is handled. The pastor in turn holds the staff members accountable for how well they have carried out their responsibilities in their specific ministry areas. The board, and others, also have set the boundaries within which the pastor and the pastor's staff must function and carry out their responsibilities. This group does not interfere with the day-to-day (or even month-to-month) running of the congregation or attempt to micromanage the ministries of the pastor and the pastor's staff.

The third major issue is that the pastor and staff members must turn the ministry back over to the laity (by equipping the saints for the work of the ministry) and the laity turn the leadership of the congregation back over to the pastor. One example of making this exchange happen means recognizing that the term "pastoral care" is an unbiblical one. At the same time, the term "congregational care" is quite biblical.

The bottom line is that the board (the lay group of people that oversees the congregation) governs (holds the pastor accountable for the mission and vision and sets the boundaries within which the leader functions), the pastor leads, the staff members manage ministry, and the congregation conducts ministry.

Conclusion of the First Lay Training

An outward-focused mission and vision, the development of intentional relationships, ministries that are staff-led, and a structure that demands accountability are all required to create a new life cycle. When these things occur and are in alignment, the congregation has the chance to experience new life. This new life cycle will once again allow the congregation to see God use it to accomplish great things in the community. A new life cycle also will enable any congregation to make many new disciples for Jesus Christ.

Making the Great Commission the Value of the Congregation

Introduction

If the purpose of the church of Jesus Christ is to make disciples, then fulfilling the Great Commission must be the value that drives all that the congregation does. Sadly, this is usually not true even for larger congregations. Any mission will only be accomplished, however, in proportion to the entity's alignment of resources to accomplish that mission. This day of training is intended to teach congregations how to align their resources to fulfill the Great Commission, assuming they see it as the mission of the church of Jesus Christ.

This day of training is divided into two major sections. The first section relates to the basic beliefs about the Great Commission that affect our behaviors in implementing it. In this section we deal first with the issue of belief (do we really believe the Great Commission is the purpose for which the church of Jesus Christ exists)? The second issue relates to leadership. If the leader of the congregation is not both convinced of this belief and modeling it, the value will not be implemented. The next issue relates to culture—how Christians view culture, and what beliefs about culture allow us to do or not do in order to fulfill the Great Commission. The fourth issue relates to our sociological understanding of how the Great Commission is accomplished. The last issue is related to the methods we use to actually carry out the Great Commission.

The second part of the training is the development of an overall congregational strategy for practicing the behavior of making disciples. Congregations have four mission fields that God is calling them to reach:

1. Those in your congregation who are not yet disciples of Jesus Christ

2. Those in your community who are like you but not yet disciples

3. Those in your community who are not like you and are not yet disciples

4. Those in other parts of the nation or the world who are not yet disciples

I take each of these four mission fields and share examples of different tactics that congregations have used to make disciples in each one.

Part One—the Belief Issue

All of us live out what we "really" believe (not what we say we believe). Therefore we must begin with what we believe the foundational purpose of the church of Jesus Christ is. Let me say at this point that God has created all things to bring glory to God. Therefore the church of Jesus Christ brings glory to God when it accomplishes its purpose. The debate, then, is over what that purpose is.

I have already stated that I believe Jesus shared that purpose the first time he mentioned the church to his disciples in Matthew 16:18. Its purpose is to defeat the aims of the Evil One. I think the Apostle Paul confirms this in the grand chapter on the church (Ephesians 3) when he states that God is glorified as God brings together two very different groups (Jews and Gentiles) in this new entity called the church. That is why the same apostle says that he and us have been given a ministry of reconciliation (2 Cor. 5:16-21). He also states that he couldn't care less that the motivation of those preaching the gospel is that Paul is in prison, as long as people become new disciples of Jesus Christ (Phil. 1:12-18). The same person tells us that Jesus Christ has two bodies (Eph. 4:4). In his first body (which he still has, though it is now a resurrected one) he came to do the will of the Father, which was to provide redemption for the world. That purpose has not changed in his second body, which is the church.

If all of this is true, then those of us who claim to be part of the church of Jesus Christ must ask ourselves a major question. This question is fundamental to all that is happening or not happening in those three continents (Europe, North America, Australia/New Zealand) most touched by the Protestant Reformation, where today the church of Jesus Christ is dying. The question is this:

Is the church of Jesus Christ a missional entity, or is it an organization with a mission statement?

If we choose the second option, which is how most congregations and denominations answer (as demonstrated by their behaviors), then eventually the demands of the organization will overtake the mission. If the former option is the one we choose, then everything becomes subject to the mission, including our denomination, our forms of acting and worshiping, our music, and so on. Our denominations and congregations are dying because we have lost the sense of mission and are no longer joining God in God's mission for the church of Jesus Christ.

Part One—the Leadership Issue

Those leading congregations to be missional are automatically involved in two cross-cultural situations. Our nation is now in essence a pagan one, which means that the church of Jesus Christ is viewed by most as irrelevant. This demands that pastors behave like missionaries who in turn teach those in the congregation to think and behave as missionaries.

The second cross-cultural situation is the congregation itself. Most people in most congregations think that their congregation exists to serve their needs. They do not see the congregation whose purpose is to use its resources (people and money) to reach others. The congregation, in the minds of most of those attending, is not seen as a place for them to be mobilized to reach their world. Congregations often lose sight of the fact that the church seeks to meet their spiritual needs, not as a end unto itself, but to prepare them to meet the needs of those who face the greatest spiritual need, life without Jesus Christ. We feed armies so they can fight, not so they can have a fine dining experience.

These cross-cultural elements demand that pastors lead the congregation to be outward in its orientation, focusing more on those who are not yet disciples of Jesus Christ than on themselves. The pastor then leads members of the congregation to act as missionaries, both corporately and individually. Pastors need to model that they themselves are making disciples in their contacts with individuals outside the church. Also, pastors need to realize that they have a continual, unrelenting responsibility to keep their congregations focused outward. This task is almost impossible in a Christian culture where there is so much focus on believers at the expense of all other concerns. One of the common mantras often heard from those in outward-focused congregations is "what about us, we have needs too." The pastors in GHC who have led their congregations to focus outward realize that the decision to be outward must be revisited every three to four years in an intentional way. If that decision is not consciously evaluated with regularity, the congregation moves back to being inwardly focused. Such a continual review will not occur if the pastor does not intentionally address the need.

Part One—the Cultural Issue

Since the beginning of the church of Jesus Christ, Christians have wrestled with how to live and interact with the culture. Much of the content in the Apostle Paul's writing discusses how Christianity is different from and yet related to Old Testament Judaism. How Christians were to interact with God's laws and teachings and yet live effectively in the culture has always created a dilemma for Christians. Perhaps the bottom line question in terms of being missional is, Does the culture in which a congregation finds itself enhance the communication of the gospel message or hinder it? Those who see the culture as friendly to communicating the message eventually face becoming so assimilated into the culture that the gospel message becomes lost and irrelevant. On the other hand, those who see the culture as an enemy in communicating the message are in danger of becoming so irrelevant and withdrawn from the culture that they lose any platform for reaching people.

I would like to suggest that the best way to deal with this is to realize that culture is neither moral nor immoral, but amoral. If culture could be described as "the normal ways people relate to each other," then culture existed before the world was ever created. God the Father has eternally generated the Son, and the Spirit eternally proceeds from both the Father and the Son. This is the normal relationship within the Trinity for all eternity. Also, God established normal ways for Adam and Eve to relate to each other and with Him prior to the Fall and the entrance of sin into creation. If this is true, then culture only becomes either moral or immoral depending on how it is employed.

This understanding about culture is important because Christians sometimes are afraid of sinning by becoming too involved in the culture, thereby limiting mission and outreach. For example, I grew up in an environment where people in my church would not even think of eating a meal with a non-Christian in a restaurant on a Sunday, even if such a meeting might help this non-Christian become a disciple of Jesus Christ. Paying for any service on a Sunday was considered sinful and a compromise with a sinful culture.

I believe that when the culture is seen as amoral, then it allows for great freedom in conducting the mission God calls the church to fulfill. For example, we have seen God work in a number of our new church starts when members have gone to bars and taverns and handed out shot glasses with the words "give us a shot" and the congregation's logo printed on them. This tactic has resulted in many unbelievers coming to the new church and becoming disciples of Jesus Christ. In one case it resulted in a congregation opening a new campus in a heavy metal bar. From twelve noon to one p.m. the culture of that bar has moved from immoral to moral in how it is being used.

Now, where God clearly condemns cultural behaviors, we cannot compromise. For example, we cannot justify lying, immorality, or stealing to advance the spread of the good news. But where the Bible is unclear, we have great latitude.

Part One—the Sociological Issues

Whenever I use the term "evangelism" people seem to automatically think of a strategy or tactic. Usually the tactics that come to the minds of people reflect two major ways in which evangelism can be implemented. One tactic is when an individual disciple of Jesus Christ shares one-on-one with another person who is not a disciple and encourages him or her in some fashion to believe the gospel message and embrace Jesus Christ as their Savior and Lord. (This particular tactic is modeled in the New Testament and has been used for over two thousand years in the church of Jesus Christ). The second tactic is where someone gets up and speaks to a crowd of people, many of whom have been invited to hear the speaker by disciples of Jesus Christ. The speaker explains the gospel message and urges those who are not followers of Jesus

Christ to respond to an invitation to embrace Jesus Christ. This model too was used in the New Testament and has been used throughout the history of the church. The basic sociological principle involved in both of these tactics assumes that disciples are establishing relationships with those who are not disciples and then leveraging those relationships to encourage people to follow Jesus Christ.

This sociological principle of bringing people to Jesus Christ on the basis of relationships is obviously a good one and probably the most basic and effective method used throughout the history of the church. Yet the use of this principle (though an excellent one) is not working in our culture because disciples for the most part are afraid or unwilling to establish such relationships and then use them to make new disciples for Jesus Christ. Therefore I think we need to think of another sociological principle we can use to help us establish relationships with those not disciples and create relevant environments where such people are open to an invitation to follow Jesus Christ.

Jesus described the making of new disciples as "fishing for men and women." Too often when we think of reaching people we think of what I call "rod and reel" fishing. By this I mean one person is responsible for developing a relationship with another person, hoping to introduce that individual to Jesus Christ while praying that such a person may then want to become a follower of Jesus Christ as a result of the introduction. This is what the terms "evangelism" or "making disciples" brings to mind for many people. Again let me reaffirm that this process works because it is the most basic sociological process in getting someone to embrace an idea, a value, a friend, a product, or a belief. However, since most Christians do not maintain relationships outside the church or are unwilling to mine the relationships they have, we need to think of another metaphor that works for such individuals. I am suggesting that the other metaphor is "net fishing." By "net fishing" I am suggesting relevant and meaningful ways for Christians to invite friends, neighbors, or co-workers to an event where relationships can be developed, yet at this event or in a series of follow-up events those who are invited are introduced to Jesus Christ and eventually invited to become a follower of Jesus Christ. We often refer to such events as bridge events. Things like Easter egg hunts, harvest fests, or living nativities enable people to invite friends to things that are not spiritually threatening in order to begin to develop relationships that can be leveraged to invite people to follow Jesus Christ.

There is one other sociological (and theological) issue that is crucial to seeing people become disciples of Jesus Christ. That is the issue of actually inviting people to believe in Jesus Christ. In some religious traditions the doctrine of God's sovereignty has so overshadowed the belief in human responsibility that people are never invited to believe. In other traditions the belief in human dignity and a fear of proselytizing has caused people never to invite others to believe. What is interesting is that while Jesus was here on earth he constantly invited people to believe in him and follow him. Even after raising Lazarus and declaring that he was the resurrection and the life, he invited both Mary and Martha to believe. The Apostle Paul invited and believed that we should persuade and constrain women and men to believe. Too often in our culture we have confused inviting with coercive tactics. As a result we will not do what Jesus did, which is invite people to believe. I find that many people love to put out bait to fish for men and women but will not set hooks in order to catch the fish.

Part Two—the Four Mission Fields

Every congregation has four mission fields to reach. The first one is the people who come to the congregation every week who are not yet disciples of Jesus Christ. The second one is the people who live in the community who are like the people in the congregation but do not attend church and are not disciples. The third is the people in the community who are not like the people in the congregation and do not attend any church. The fourth mission field is the people in the nation and around the world who are not disciples of Jesus Christ.

In this part of the training we suggest various strategies and tactics for reaching these various mission fields.

Part Two—the First Mission Field

The first mission field is the people who actually show up on Sunday and attend the service. This is the easiest and least expensive mission field to reach since the people come to the congregation. It is often the most ignored since many assume that if people come they must already be disciples or somehow will become disciples on their own initiative without any help from anyone in the congregation.

The main tactic I suggest for this mission field is to intentionally develop a presentation in the connecting or assimilating process where people are both introduced to Jesus Christ and then invited to become a disciple. I also suggest that those in the congregation to whom God has given the gift of evangelism be the ones to offer this invitation.

Part Two—the Second Mission Field

The second mission field is the people in the community who are like the people in the congregation (ethnically, economically, socially, and the like) but do not attend church. These are the people we (the congregation) participate with in our civic life, people who usually live in the same neighborhoods as we do.

At this point we discuss strategies related to bridge events, friendship evangelism, and other means for reaching those who are like us. We also discuss special Sundays and other kinds of church events that enable us to invite these individuals to participate with us and get to know us.

Part Two—the Third Mission Field

The third mission field is the people in the community who are not like the people in the congregation. In a nation that has a broad middle class (lower middle, middle, and upper middle), this often means reaching out to either the powerless and those without resources in the culture and those who are the most powerful and resourceful in the culture, the wealthy people. Reaching this mission field successfully usually means that most who become disciples of Jesus Christ will never regularly attend the congregation that reached out to them. The purpose of reaching this mission field is to build God's kingdom, not the local congregation.

Each congregation should create an environment that generates a group of "spiritual entrepreneurs" who create ministries that are designed to engage the people not like us in their environments. The purpose of these ministries, especially to those without power and resources, is not only to touch the physical needs they live with constantly but ultimately to touch their spiritual need to have a living and redemptive encounter with the resurrected Lord Jesus Christ.

Part Two—the Fourth Mission Field

The fourth mission field is the people outside our community who are not disciples of Jesus Christ. Historically this mission field has been known as national and international missions. There are a host of denominational and para-church agencies designed to reach different kinds of people within this vast mission field. Yet we believe that God directs each congregation to reach a piece of this mission field as well.

The main strategy we discuss is the development of short-term mission teams who leave their homes and communities to engage in helping reach a particular segment of this mission field. We encourage such teams to do their mission work with those who are in cultures that have far fewer resources than the congregation. When we send mission teams to such places, the members gain a greater awareness of the material and spiritual needs of people in their *own* communities—and hence understand why the church needs to be focused outward.

Conclusion

The last part of the strategy is two lay training events for the congregations in which the pastors are participating in clusters or learning communities and in which consultations have taken place. The purpose is to bring on board an even wider group of people to support a transformation from being inward-focused as a congregation to becoming outward-focused.

The first training event is to help the congregation understand that God has called the church of Jesus Christ to be a missional entity that is designed more to reach those who are not yet disciples than to be an organization of comfort for those who are already disciples. It shows those attending how to move from being inward-focused to being outward-focused.

The second training event teaches laity to place making disciples of Jesus Christ at the core of the congregation's values. Theological issues are discussed along with other key understandings. Specific strategies and tactics are also presented to show how to reach the four mission fields we believe each congregation is called to serve.

CHAPTER SEVEN
Military Advisers

Tess and her husband had the potential to be a very good pastoral lead-ership team. She had good organizational and management skills. He had the ability to relate to people well and to provide the social glue that enabled individuals to follow the ideas Tess proposed. There were only two major problems. First, neither Tess nor her husband knew how to lead a growing congregation. Second, Tess and her husband did not see themselves as leaders or people needing to exercise leadership behavior. As a result their congregation was small, was not growing, and the lead-ership vacuum had been taken over by others in the congregation.

Tess's denomination offered her and her husband a weekend consultation with the promise of walking alongside the congregation if the people voted to embrace the prescriptions. She and her husband agreed and the week-end went very well. As a result she and her husband joined a pastoral learning community led by a mentor, were assigned a congregational coach, and each was teamed with a personal coach for a year.

Tess already had a coach. Unfortunately that coach had no effective pas-toral experience and had no idea how to help her lead the congregation through the transformation process and in turn help the congregation grow. Tess's denomination connected her with two female executive pas-tors in larger congregations. Tess asked one of these individuals to become her new coach and a bond was soon formed between these two women.

Because of her gifts, Tess began to become much more dominant in lead-ing the congregation. As a result, some people began to resist. They rec-ognized that change was really going to occur, that Tess was becoming more and more of the leader (which for some was not what they wanted), and that many of their older traditions would be going by the wayside in order to reach out to new people.

Tess's phone calls with her coach became quite intense as she was taught how to both implement new ideas and deal with those people who were doing everything they could to stop the changes. Tess and her husband began to rely even more heavily on their learning community mentor, sit-uational coaches, and congregational coach to navigate the deep waters

they were facing. Eventually the changes took root, the people who needed to leave the congregation left, and a whole flood of new people began to arrive as the revitalized congregation started to grow and reproduce.

Now both Tess and her husband will tell you the changes would not have occurred and they would not have made it to the other side of the transformation process without the help of their personal coaches, the congregational coach, and their mentor. These people were crucial since they had all "been there," "done that," and knew how to help others go through what they had experienced successfully.

Introduction

A new term has come into our vocabulary in my lifetime: "military adviser." My understanding is that a military adviser is someone who has become an outstanding soldier because of having been effective in military endeavors. This person is then assigned to work with other military people, often from other countries, to help them learn how to engage their enemies effectively and successfully. The goal of military advisers is to help other soldiers accomplish their mission well.

The new "in" term in the business world is "coach." Again, this person, like a military adviser, is someone who comes alongside another individual or group and helps them achieve their personal or collective mission.

Advisers, coaches, mentors, consultants, and the like are not new. Such people have been around since the beginning of time. People who have learned some information, skill, process, or behavior have passed that knowledge on to others. Someone had to teach Cain how to farm and Abel how to shepherd. This learning came from their parents, who, as any good parents do, coach, advise, train, consult, and correct their children. The Bible also describes this process with the term "disciple." A disciple is basically a learner who learns from someone more advanced and experienced in that which is being learned.

For many years the culture of the church has been to create independent contractors who function on their own. Pastors too often see themselves in competition with other pastors and as a result cut themselves off from learning those best practices that peers might teach them. As people go to college and seminary, they learn to function in a highly individual manner and then bring that independent mindset into the pastorate. Some may see the need to read and attend conferences and seminars. Even the pastors who are willing to learn, though, often see themselves as independent implementers of that which is learned. And as denominational people have had less and less to teach, often because they do not know what to teach or do not have the experience from which to teach, pastors feel very much on their own. They still maintain collegial connections for fellowship and friendship, but not for learning.

Added to this independent mindset is the fact that most pastors are not leaders in an environment that calls them to at least demonstrate leadership behaviors. The combination of these two concepts—independence in learning and hesitancy to be leaders—contributes to most pastors never implementing well that which they do know or that which they really wish to accomplish.

Thus, coaches, mentors, consultants, and advisers are needed until the denomination can create an environment of peer learning. It is important that those filling these teaching or training roles be women and men of effective and successful experience who communicate from a foundation of experiential knowledge, not just theoretical or academic learning. And even once a peer learning environment has been created, such people are still needed, due to the speed of change and the increasing amount of information generated in this culture.

The Concept of Coaching

Coaching has been going on from the beginning of history. In most ancient cultures men taught their sons how to farm, hunt, fish, work, and act within the community, while women taught their daughters how to cook, clean, and act within the community. In the middle ages the coaching process took a more organized form called apprenticeship. Master craftsmen would employ young people for labor and in exchange give them formal training in their craft. While schools had been around since ancient times, the teaching process became more formal with the rise of what are today called universities.

Coaching as a discipline began in the late 1930s in the U.S. but became far more formal in the 1990s with the rise of numerous self-appointed advisers and self-regulating bodies. Today there are life coaches, business coaches, executive coaches, personal coaches, spiritual coaches, health coaches, financial coaches, media coaches, birth coaches, and even dating coaches. In some business environments having a coach is a requirement for peer and supervisor approval and even advancement. We live today in a coaching culture.

While "coaching" has become faddish in some ways, the concept is not new and it will always be with us. Experienced people sharing their knowledge and expertise with people who are less knowledgeable or experienced is a way of life. The fact that we are now more intentional about coaching is good, particularly in areas like congregational life, where so many pastors have become independent operators, to the detriment of their congregations and themselves.

The Relationship between Coaching and Mentoring

Some people attempt to draw sharp distinctions between "coaching" and "mentoring." There are, however, far more similarities than differences between the two. Both involve passing on knowledge and experience. Both seek to empower others by helping the recipients become more effective and successful. Both take advantage of the "teachable moment," since they are done in the area where "the game is being played." Both coaching and mentoring use the tool of self-discovery to help people gain wisdom and insight from their behaviors, whether such behaviors are appropriate or inappropriate. Finally, good mentors and coaches are willing to confront those they are helping and can often do it effectively, since as a coach or mentor they have established good relationships with the person being coached or mentored.

In reality, coaching and mentoring attempt to accomplish the same things. Coaching is an athletic metaphor, while mentoring comes from the educational world. The chart below may reveal some subtle differences in how these disciplines are employed:

Distinctions between Coaching and Mentoring	
Coaching (Athletic Metaphor)	Mentoring (Educational Metaphor)
More an authority figure	More a parent figure or friend
More invested in team	More invested in individual
More coach-to-players	More one-on-one
More action-oriented	More knowledge-oriented
More specific—tasks, issues	More comprehensive life
More professional	More intimate
More "for a season"	More "for a lifetime"
Sometimes not a good player	Usually a good player
From the sidelines	On the field
Coach as expert	Mentor as practitioner

Coaching and Mentoring in Growing Healthy Churches

The strategy developed in this book is based upon all that God is teaching us about transformation in our region called Growing Healthy Churches. Therefore I want to explain our environment and then detail how our learning relates to the strategy I am sharing with other denominations.

Overview

We use three forms of coaching and mentoring. First, we provide mentoring in the context of peer-to-peer mentoring clusters (often called learning communities in other denominations). We define a cluster mentor as a person who engages in a long-term relationship with a group of pastors (or staff members). The purpose for this relationship is to develop their pastoral leadership skills, encourage them as they make key and often tough decisions, and help them gain in their overall ability to lead a congregation. We ask our mentors to help pastors establish both personal and professional goals for which they are held accountable.

Second, we provide coaching. Coaching is a one-on-one relationship between a peer with proven experience in developing and using leadership skills and another person needing to develop such skills. The coach's role is to enable the pastor to gain proficiency in developing and employing pastoral leadership skills. The coach helps the person he or she is coaching define the key issues and challenges they are facing, identify possible solutions, and then lead that individual to execute a strategy for implementing the changes required.

Third, we also provide congregational coaching. Most coaching focuses on the individual leader and his or her professional growth. Congregational coaching focuses on the "leadership community" and the ability of that community to lead the congregation. The congregational coach normally works with this leadership community after a consultation in order to help them implement the changes prescribed in the consultation.

P2P² Coaching and Mentoring

Early on in the transformation process in GHC, we began to change the way our pastoral clusters were led. We had already changed the content from fellowship and prayer to training in congregational health, leadership, and spiritual formation. The change in leadership was that instead of assigning regional staff to lead the clusters, we asked pastors to do so. Experience has taught us that mentoring and coaching (with rare exceptions) need to be led by full-time practitioners who are part-time mentors and coaches. Such peer-to-peer (P2P) coaching and mentoring is not only the best way to go; it is financially the most feasible for denominations.

However, true peer-to-peer relationships will not work if those leading or organizing the clusters and learning communities do not excel in their experience over the rest of the pastors or staff members in the group. These groups will eventually end up pooling their ignorance and reaching the lowest common denominator of learning and produce no accountable behaviors that lead to systemic change.

Therefore P2P mentoring is not sufficient. Coaching and mentoring that brings about transformational change in the lives of pastors, lay leaders, and congregation requires $P2P^2$ ("peer-to-peer squared") mentoring and coaching. By this I mean that the pastors doing the mentoring and coaching must have demonstrated greater effectiveness and growth in leading their congregations than the ones they are coaching and mentoring. It also means that these effective pastors are holding the pastors in the clusters accountable for measurable goals. Without accountability, few pastors and congregations will experience transformation.

All of these concepts are part of the various elements in the strategy being described in this book and that I am using with denominations. Part one of the strategy is putting those pastors in the experimental group into a cluster or learning community. During the consultation weekend often one of the prescriptions (or at least one piece of one prescription) is to say that the pastor must engage a coach. Then as the denomination walks alongside a congregation, assuming the congregation has embraced the prescriptions in the report, that congregation is assigned a congregational coach.

I also teach and expect the denominations I am working with to choose only effective pastors of larger congregations to lead the clusters and conduct both kinds of coaching. This means that, in the more connectional denominations, people who hold judicatory power over the congregations cannot fulfill either coaching role if they do not have the experiential credentials. The judicatory representative's role is to support both coaches and the pastor, not to represent the congregation during the process of transformation.

Clusters, or Learning Communities

I have talked previously about the clusters, or learning communities, since they are the first part of the strategy. Here I would like to discuss different kinds of clusters, since we are constantly experimenting in our region. We have reinvented our cluster system three times in ten years and are always trying new ways to deliver training to our pastors and congregations. Normally our clusters meet once a month. This means that the clusters and the mentors leading those clusters are the primary source of training for our pastors in leadership and congregational health. We do other kinds of clusters and large events to support that which is occurring in the clusters. However, the pastoral clusters are always fundamental to how we train.

In most cases clusters are comprised of five to ten pastors, with the leader being called a mentor pastor. Our mentors are compensated and are expected to hold the pastors accountable. The advantages to conducting training this way are that group dynamics contribute to the learning and the training is economically feasible. Also, mentors learn to develop into more effective pastors as they teach others.

Generally in our region we have created clusters based on geography, as opposed to other considerations. One main reason is that geographic clusters are our tradition, but there are others. Proximity and reduced travel time for the pastors involved is one major advantage. Also, as our pastors become much more collegial in their relationships, rather than being competitive, they develop greater interaction with each other and with their congregations. Often in such cases there is more of a shared cultural context among congregations, although that is not always true in Northern California. The best advantage is that the more effective pastors can contribute to the training atmosphere, providing encouragement and expertise for those pastors who are not as effective in ministry.

The primary disadvantage arises out of ministry diversity. Having effective pastors mixed in with ineffective pastors usually lowers the level of learning and may cause the more effective pastors to be less motivated to participate. Also, as pastors in larger contexts interact with each other, pastors in smaller congregations may be less motivated to listen since they have never experienced the issues being discussed. Also, pastors in communities that reflect greater cultural diversity may find it hard to appreciate a learning environment that attempts to meet everyone's needs.

We have also conducted affinity-based clusters. I created one cluster where the affinity was highly motivated pastors who were also quite effective in leading their congregations. Although the sizes of congregations were different, the attitude and morale of the pastors created an experience in the cluster that these pastors still talk about years later. Obviously, one key advantage to such clusters is the relevancy factor. Pastors are able to observe how the training fits them and to interact with others in similar situations to learn from their peers. Such clusters also create a sense of camaraderie and connection that may not occur in other types of clusters.

The biggest disadvantage to this kind of affinity-based cluster is that the less effective pastors lose the opportunity to learn from their more effective peers. Also, placing the less effective pastors together in clusters, which I have done in the past, creates an environment that often has no sense of momentum or excitement. The result is less learning and pastors developing their leadership skills more slowly.

Finally, we are beginning to experiment with virtual clusters. We are doing this in part because most younger pastors tend to use the Internet very differently from the majority of older pastors. Younger pastors often seem to live on the net, conducting research, reading the news, developing relationships, and so forth. Such pastors use a myriad of technologies, including instant messaging, blogs, and webinars. These pastors favor this format since it eliminates travel (and hence is more environmentally friendly), saves time and expenses, and does not have an institutional feel.

We have found that the best virtual clusters are comprised of three elements. First, there is the meeting itself, where materials are made available online, and a free-flowing conversation is conducted through various audio or visual media.

Second, the mentor follows up with a personal contact with participants to discuss how the training is going, or how it will impact their ministry context. While virtual clusters can develop a real sense of community for people who live this way, it is difficult to ensure that accountability takes place. That is why such follow-up by the mentor is crucial, because without accountability and encouragement, change often does not occur.

Third, effective virtual clusters make use of e-mail, text messages, phone calls, and blogs between participants between meetings. While other types of clusters may use these means, in virtual clusters they are critical, since they reflect the primary way that training is delivered, community is maintained, peer-to-peer learning occurs, and accountability is ensured.

Virtual clusters require mentors who are not only effective pastors but who live on the web and are effective communicators in using this vast and complex tool. It also means that participants must be even more committed to maintaining the learning relationships, since they are not sitting down in one place at a certain time to meet face-to-face with people.

The strategy being developed in this book means that judicatories or associations will need to establish more and more clusters each year. The pastors in the initial cluster will want to continue, and other clusters will need to be established as more congregations get involved in the process. Therefore the judicatory will need to plan ahead to determine the kinds of clusters or learning communities they want to establish. Each judicatory may need to do it differently so it fits their situation. The only absolute I insist on is to not place any pastor in a cluster who is not part of the process. Doing so will have a long-term detrimental effect, since you will soon end up with pastors who are not motivated and who will not be held accountable.

Mentors as Leaders

The mentors in GHC are very special people. They are first of all effective men and women who demonstrate leadership in their families and in their ministries. We have invested heavily in their training to be both pastors and mentors. As a result they lead their clusters effectively. These women and men set the agenda for their individual clusters. In most contexts they decide on the teaching topics, the books and resources that will be used, and the structure of each meeting. At times we have created a curriculum for mentors to use. Even then the mentors have been free to use or not use what we have created. They are also given wide latitude in how they will use any material we have created. After all, these people are leaders, they are committed to the mission and vision of GHC, and they constantly communicate the DNA of GHC.

I and our coach to the mentors make sure that over time each mentor provides training in leadership and congregational health and growth, works on the spiritual formation of pastors, helps them with self care for both themselves and their families, develops community among those within the cluster, and provides accountability for personal and professional growth.

Effective leaders take responsibility, live responsibly, and hold others accountable. Therefore, effective mentors take responsibility for their clusters. In addition to that which happens in the cluster, they take responsibility for participation. They also personally invite new pastors to be involved, as well as pastors from other denominations in their area. When pastors miss, they check on them in order to see if they are dealing with issues that the mentor might be able to help them face and handle effectively. Also, there are times when the mentor and the mentor's congregation might help someone in the cluster with some resources that may enhance the ministry of his or her congregation.

Our mentors also model that they are willing to live responsibly themselves. They handle issues and problems in their congregations with honesty and integrity, even if it is to their own detriment. They read far more books than most pastors in their clusters. They attend seminars and training events both within GHC and across the nation.

Our mentors lead by holding pastors within their clusters accountable. They do not set the pastor's goals, since that would encourage them to act like parents. Rather, they expect each pastor to set goals in both the pastor's personal and professional lives. The mentor then interacts with the pastors periodically to see how progress is being made in achieving the goals. If pastors do not set goals or if they consistently fail to reach their goals, then the mentors lead by asking them to no longer be involved in the cluster.

Let me add quickly at this point that, as Baptists, neither I nor the mentors have authority over any pastor. Therefore such accountability as I am describing cannot be compelled. It comes as people are led to embrace this accountability on their own. That only happens because our clusters are so effective and our mentors so respected that people are willing to place themselves under accountability in order to be a part of this training process. Pastors follow the mentors who lead first by example.

Coaching

In GHC we define coaching as a one-on-one relationship between a person with skills, experience, and insight (the coach) who helps the person being coached to more clearly define the issues and challenges they are facing, helps that individual identify possible solutions to the situation, and then provides guidance in developing a path for the effective implementation of a strategy to handle well the situation at hand.

Many forms of coaching cause the coach and the person being coached to develop a long-term relationship. Life coaches, personal coaches, and spiritual coaches (often called spiritual directors) all tend to work with a client on a wide range of issues over time. These coaches often direct their clients across a broad spectrum of personal, professional, and organizational issues over an extended period of time. In GHC this kind of coaching is usually handled by mentors in the context of the cluster system. That is not to say that what coaches do is wrong; it is simply to say that we cover many of these areas through our mentors.

In GHC we tend to use more of a situational approach. In fact we use the term "situational coaching" to express what we do. Situational coaching is more short-term and is focused on a particular challenge, opportunity, or relationship the congregation or pastor is facing. Typically, situational coaching arrangements last between four and twelve sessions.

We have developed this way of coaching in part because we have such an effective mentor system. However, we have also developed situational coaching, since the normal type of coaching requires people with superior skills in coaching across a wide range of areas of expertise. And while these coaches may have great background and skills, they often do not have the kind of effective pastoral leadership experience required to help our pastors lead effective change. On the other hand, there are many effective pastors who have the kind of experiential background our pastors need who can also provide significant short-term help. Such people often do not see themselves as coaches, and yet they know how to help because they have done it. Some who are quite capable leaders who always seem to react well may not be good coaches. However, there are many effective pastors who have had to think their way through tough issues. These leaders may make great situational coaches and pass along many of the thinking and ministry skills they have developed in the crucible of ministry.

During the first session the situational coach seeks to clarify the issues, needs, or challenges that accompany the issues. The coach then determines whether she or he can provide the help being requested. If so, the coaching session proceeds, with the coach determining whether the needs presented are the real issues or symptoms that reflect a greater problem. Identifying the foundational problem is the first real step in dealing with any issue. The coach then makes one or two assignments. If more data is required, the coach asks that such data be collected and communicated to the coach. The coach may also begin to have the pastor develop the resources required to deal effectively with the issue at hand.

The next several sessions involve the identification of several solutions and then the creation of an action plan. This action plan needs to delineate the specific steps that are to be taken in arriving at a solution. It is imperative to have the person being coached move to action as soon as possible, in order to demonstrate that progress is occurring. Situational coaching is not therapy. It is practical, pragmatic, and action-oriented.

In the sessions following the development and implementation of an action plan, the coach holds the pastor accountable for the actions taken. Time is also spent evaluating the actions in order to ascertain that they have been implemented with wisdom, and whether some changes in the plan are required in light of responses to the actions taken. If the pastor gets stuck, the coach helps the pastor get unstuck by talking through the experiences and drawing on the coach's wisdom to provide solutions to meet the current and immediate need.

Each session includes a reporting and a debriefing process so the coach and the pastor are clear about that which is and is not happening. Continual adjustments are made until there is some form of resolution and the problem is addressed effectively. Once that happens, the coach releases the pastor from the coaching relationship, since the coach's expertise is no longer required.

Coaching and the Strategy

I have taken time to discuss how we come at coaching in GHC in order to explain how this fits into the strategy being described. As previously stated, I usually require the pastor to employ a coach for at least one year. I see this as a yearlong situational coaching relationship that will help the pastor address the issues related to initial transformation and create action steps to deal with those issues.

Therefore, I usually assign coaches who have led dying or declining congregations through the steps required to experience an initial transformation of the entire system. These people realize how difficult it is to keep the momentum going that has been generated by the weekend consultation. They understand that pressure will come from a number of dissatisfied individuals in the congregation who do not want any changes that will upset their status, challenge their traditions, or make them uncomfortable. These coaches know that initial transformation is one of the most difficult tasks a pastor will ever perform, and that most pastors are not trained or equipped to lead this task on their own. This is also the time when support for the pastor and the pastor's family is usually required.

The coach is working with a pastor who is leading a congregation from death to life. It will take at least a year. It will mean implementing the prescriptions from the consultation, as well as other changes. It will require a lot of listening, numerous strategies requiring many action steps, and the wisdom and insight that can only come from those who have done it well. At this point, the pastor does not need a life coach or some other kind of long-term coaching experience. The pastor may need and want such coaches later. However, at this point the pastor *needs* a situational coach who has "been there, done that" and seen success.

Congregational Coaching

In situational and life coaching the client is the individual pastor or leader. In congregational coaching the client is the congregation, and the coach works with the "leadership community." By "leadership community" I mean the senior pastor, staff members (whether they are paid full or part-time staff or are volunteers), key lay leaders of key ministries, and the board (or council or whatever the lay governing body is called).

In larger congregations a defined group of individuals selected from all these categories are the people with whom the coach works.

The congregational coach works with the congregation for one year once it has accepted the consultation prescriptions. This person's role, along with the pastor's coach, is to help the congregation implement the prescriptions arising from the consultation report.

Effective congregational coaches possess specific characteristics. While a coach or mentor might have some or all of these characteristics, it is almost imperative that a congregational coach have them all in order to work at maximum effectiveness.

The first criterion is one that has been emphasized throughout the strategy. They must possess effective transformation experience. They cannot be theoreticians or academics when it comes to leading a congregation through its initial transformation from death to life. Their knowledge must come from having gone through the heat of battle and thrived while doing so. This is why many middle judicatory people, even those with close connectional ties to pastors and congregations, cannot be the one who walks alongside a congregation for a year. Unless they have led a congregation through transformation and as a result seen that congregation grow and get past the two-hundred barrier, they cannot coach in this way. They simply do not have the skills and experience to act as coaches.

Effective congregational coaches must also possess a wide range of experiences. It is best if they have provided effective pastoral leadership to more than one congregation (they need to be more than a one-trick pony). They need to have led congregations that are larger than the one they are coaching. They themselves should have a history of being coached or mentored (they know how to listen, receive advice, and then implement it). They have good peer relationships with other effective pastors and those serving in specialized fields of ministry (youth, children, assimilation). They also should have some cross-cultural experience that has taught them to think like missionaries. Often, great solutions to key issues come from those who can think outside the cultural box in which they live and minister.

These effective coaches also understand congregational systems. They understand how all the systems in the congregation contribute to one big, effective system. However, they also understand all the subsystems because they themselves established effective systems when they were leading a congregation. But beyond understanding systems, these coaches are system thinkers. By this I mean they realize how every change will affect numerous entities throughout all the systems of the congregation, not just the one on which they are focused at a certain point in time. They have the ability to both analyze and synthesize, so they see both the forest and the trees.

These coaches possess a confident humility that gives them the ability to confront and stand strong in the face of resistance. They know both when and how to draw lines in the sand. They also know when and where to compromise without watering down the stands they have taken and continue to take. Behaving this way demands wisdom, humility, and a strong confidence in oneself, because of how God has led this person to act in the past.

Finally, these people must posses the ability to teach and communicate what they have learned and not be threatened by resistance and rejection. There are times when all the different groups within the leadership community will react negatively to the coach, because they themselves are fearful and usually do not see the big picture. A good coach anticipates these reactions and is prepared to walk people through these difficult times without taking their responses personally.

Few people fit all the criteria I have described, but there are many who come close. And there are people like this in most communities, or at least close enough to most congregations to be a coach. The problem is they are often not in the denomination with which I am working. This means that these denominations must go outside their tribe to recruit such people to work with their pastors and congregations. The coach is in a place to help the congregation's leaders implement effectively the prescriptions coming out of the consultation. Therefore, with good coaches it does not matter what the denomination of the congregation is. Good coaches can help that congregation become effective in its cultural and religious context.

Situational and Congregational Coaches

In the best of situations both the situational coach and the congregational coach work as a team, because they are working on the same issue of overall transformation. One is focusing on the pastor and the pastor's role, while the other is focusing on the congregation in general and the leadership community in particular. "If both coaches are attempting to accomplish the same thing," someone might ask, "then why are both needed?" While this is a fair observation and critique, let me assure you that both coaches are needed, particularly since the coaches need to deal with the stresses placed on the pastor and the pastor's family as a result of leading the transformation process.

First, the level of pastoral leadership in many congregations is so low that, to offer pastors hope of succeeding and their congregations the hope of being effective, as many human resources as possible should work with the pastor, the pastor's family, and the congregation. Many pastors not only struggle with not knowing what to do, they struggle equally with not knowing how to accomplish the what. It is not just a matter of giving pastors the right information but guiding them through the use and implementation of that information. One reason we see so many pastors become highly effective is that we surround them with effective coaches.

Second, no coach functions full-time with the person they are coaching. Yet a good number of pastors could benefit from such a relationship. Also, many good situational and congregational coaches are effective pastors leading their own congregations. They are coaching in a part-time role, often because they want to see God turn around other congregations. Therefore it is beneficial for the pastor and congregation being coached to have at least two people they can go to, plus the mentor in their learning community, for help when it is needed. Yet this need for help should not overburden the coaches, since they are one of several resources being employed.

Third, it may be difficult to find two coaches (the situational coach and the congregational coach) that have all the needed qualifications I have described in this book. Therefore, by having two you should have coaches who complement one another in terms of their gifting and experience.

This means that both the congregational and the situational coach work with the pastor for twelve months. The congregational coach brings one extra piece of accountability to the training, since that person is actually having monthly face-to-face encounters with the leaders of the congregation.

The congregational coach also helps the leaders prioritize the prescriptions. Even though this is usually done in the report itself, there are times when the situation in the congregation means executing, for example, prescription number three ahead of number two. Also, some prescriptions assume the pastor or others are working on things, so when the time for implementation arrives, the right resources are in place. The congregational coach makes sure that the appropriate homework is being conducted in preparation for that which is to come.

Finally, the congregational coach either brings the needed training to the congregation or makes sure that another person is recruited to provide it. The congregational coach introduces the leaders to resources, gives out assignments, hold leaders accountable, and walks with them through the trials and the successes. Finally, this coach teaches the leaders to develop a culture of accountability.

Conclusion

The world in which we live is changing rapidly every day, and knowledge is increasing at rates that are staggering. Yet the church of Jesus Christ is in decline and most pastors, lay leaders, denominational people, and seminary professors do not know what to do. Help is needed if denominations and congregations in the nations most touched by the Protestant Reformation are to avoid going the way of the dinosaurs. The good news is that such help is available, if denominations and associations will look in the right places and find the right people.

These people are the mentors, coaches, consultants, and advisers who have led congregational transformation. These are the practitioners who have practiced well and effectively, both personally and professionally. Such people need to be recruited, mobilized, and then turned loose to work with pastors and congregations.

The transformer must be transformed before those the transformer is leading can embrace transformation and be changed. This demands advisers who have been transformed themselves, both personally and professionally.

Our denominations did not get to their current state overnight. It took time. Change will take time. It involves a strategy and a process. It also means getting the right people in place to help those who need their expertise the most.

Final Notes

The research for this chapter was done by Bill Hoyt. Bill is one of those rare people who has been an effective pastor and judicatory leader and now is an effective consultant, mentor, and coach. Bill heads up the entire transformation area for GHC. His ministry of NexStep Coaching enables him to work effectively with pastors and congregations across the nation. Bill is also an effective writer; see his book *Effectiveness by the Numbers,* published by Abingdon Press. Bill may be contacted at Bill@NexStepcoaching.org.

Teresa Flint-Borden is a highly effective mentor. She specializes in helping clergy couples deal with those family issues that arise as the pastor is attempting to lead systemic change. Her therapeutic practice based upon an integration of scripture and Neuro-Transformation Relaxation Response (NTR^2) produces relief from many symptoms associated with stress. It also helps couples find new ways of behaving effectively in the midst of crisis. Her background in change and transition management, coupled with her successes in working with GHC clergy couples, provides the effective experience required for mentors and coaches. She may be contacted by e-mail at teresa@bordenspeaks.com or TeamOffice@aol.com; or by phone at 925-277-2980.

CHAPTER EIGHT
Engaging the Enemy

Working the Strategy

More than sixty pastors, lay leaders, and denominational people sat in a motel conference room in order to attempt a grand experiment. Five teams of ten people each had been assembled. These teams were planning to consult with five inner city congregations for the weekend. Each team was led by either an effective pastor or denominational leader who understood the key issues related to congregational health and growth. The rest of the team members were primarily there to observe, learn, and be trained as congregational consultants and coaches.

Each of the five congregations selected had at one time been large center-city congregations. Over the years, however, the city had changed, the congregations had declined, and several congregations were even contemplating closing.

The pastors of these congregations were now in a learning community where each month they were being trained in congregational health and leadership. They had led their congregations to be a part of this experiment and as a result each congregation had completed a self-study.

The members of the five consulting teams had been sent copies of the self-study and were expected to have read all the material and come to this event prepared to interact with each other about the congregation they were going to consult. Each member had been asked to generate a list of questions that might be asked during the weekend consultation. Each person was also to bring a list of the best strengths and primary concerns for each congregation.

This particular denomination is attempting to generate a large group of consultants. To be invited to be a consultant, though, the person must have effective congregational leadership experience. That person must then observe two consultations, help conduct two consultations with other experienced consultants, and then lead two consultations while being observed by experienced consultants. This grand experiment was designed to see if such training could be done on a large scale.

On the first day of the gathering I was asked to give an overview of both the consulting process and the content that needed to be shared during the weekend consultations. On the second day I had each team share their congregational presentations with the entire group. Each team had an hour to give an overview of the situation, what had led to the current problems, the needs that required change, and what they were going to prescribe for this congregation. I then led the entire group to interact with the team in order to hone their understanding, process, and prescriptions.

On Friday morning the groups met for the final time and then dispersed to work with the five congregations. After the weekend was over and the consultations were complete, all five teams reconvened to debrief and discuss their experiences.

The result was that all five congregations voted to embrace the prescriptions and are now in the process of turning around. This weekend experience worked so well that this denomination has repeated the experiment several times.

Introduction

The strategy described in this book is based upon that which God has been teaching us in GHC for over a decade about successful congregational transformation in order to see the turnaround in our judicatory. The strategy reflects the evolution in our thinking as we learn more and more each time we work with a congregation.

The strategy was developed in a more formal way as we were asked to work with other denominations reflecting beliefs and polities that were not Baptist or congregational. People expressed a desire to see if God would do for them what he has done and continues to do for us, without becoming us. Again, the strategy continues to evolve as we work in and with denominations that are different from us in many ways.

Therefore, I have asked four judicatory or associational leaders to share their experiences in using this strategy with their congregations. I have chosen a Lutheran denomination (The Lutheran Church—Missouri Synod). This denomination in its polity has both aspects of congregationalism and more connectional bodies. It is much more doctrinaire in its theology than American Baptists and often this theology informs how congregations function.

The second group is the Salvation Army (The Salvation Army, Southern Territory in Australia). The Army is probably the most connectional of all denominations, in many ways following a military chain of command. It is also viewed as a group highly committed to what is often referred to as social justice issues. Also, using a group outside of North America (though European in its heritage) reveals to some degree the transferability of the strategy.

The third group is the State of Florida judicatory for the Church of God, Anderson. This group, like Baptists, is congregational in polity and very fearful of any outside involvement by the judicatory or any other denominational entity.

The fourth group is the Trinity Fellowship Association of Churches. This association, not a denomination, is related to Trinity Fellowship Church in Amarillo, Texas. This megachurch of over eight thousand, like a number of other megachurches, has formed its own association of churches. It is charismatic in tradition and highly theocratic in polity.

These four examples represent wide differences in how denominations (and associations) and the congregations that make up their traditions relate to each other and in how they rule themselves. Yet like almost all denominations in Europe, North America, and Australia and New Zealand, these groups were in decline and were watching many of their congregations die. Our theologies, denominational practices, and polities may be quite different, but the challenges we face are common ones and this strategy addresses those problems.

When I asked these leaders to submit their stories, I thought I would edit what they submitted in order to make the writing throughout the book uniform. However, as I read what they wrote, I felt it was better for you to hear their voices more directly than having me interpret them to you. Also, it is important that you hear from them that which works and that which does not. As a result I am turning the rest of the chapter over to them.

Testimony 1: The Lutheran Church— Missouri Synod
By Terry Tieman[1]

Some things come into your life with equal parts joy and pain. One of those is childbirth. Another is the transformation of a judicatory. As a husband and father, I have only experienced the joy side of childbirth. As a pastor and church executive, however, I have experienced both expressions of church transformation—the joy and the pain!

As a parish pastor, God has given me the blessing of leading several churches from being plateaued or declining to growth and even reproduction. However, with no tools like *Hit the Bullseye* or *Direct Hit* available at the time, and with little help from my judicatory, there was a considerable amount of learning the hard way. This included losing members upset that "their" pastor was spending so much time with new people—often the wrong kind of people, at that—changing time-honored traditions, and continually harping about the lost and unchurched.

With the joy of kingdom growth far outweighing the pain, especially through the experience of church planting, I jumped at the chance to be the full-time Director of Missions for the Mid-South District of The Lutheran Church—Missouri Synod (LCMS) thirteen years ago. My thinking was that I would have the opportunity to plant dozens, maybe even hundreds, of new churches throughout our judicatory. After all, if our small congregation in western Arkansas could grow and plant new churches, how much more could be done across the entire district?

Over the next decade, what I found out was both exciting and frustrating. It wasn't that difficult to start new churches. Our region of about 120 churches started some 25 new missions in that period. What was difficult, however, was getting those new churches past the point where they were small and struggling. Most of the new churches stalled out after a few years of growth, gathered mainly people of Lutheran background or who were already Christians, required large sums of outside money to sustain them, and generated few conversions.

Being somewhat of a slow learner, I finally came to the conclusion that something (or somebody) needed to change. It occurred to me that the DNA of the new churches we were starting matched that of the existing churches in our judicatory. That is, they were more focused on themselves and their own needs and desires than those of their community. They were often more concerned about maintaining tradition and being in control than they were with bringing lost people into a life-saving relationship with Jesus. Unless the fundamental DNA could be changed, planting churches from this shallow gene pool would never be the catalyst for kingdom growth that I had imagined.

Of course, how that might be accomplished, I had absolutely no idea, other than to pray and hope for a miracle. The miracle came in the person and teaching of Paul Borden! A good friend of mine, who has also served as my mentor and consultant, recommended that I read Borden's book, *Hit the Bullseye*. I remember very clearly reading the entire book during a plane ride to the West Coast for a national missions conference. I was so frustrated at the time that I was considering going back into the parish ministry, where I might really be able to do some good.

But my loving and gracious God had other ideas. Borden's book really hit me between the eyes. I couldn't put it down the entire plane ride. People sitting next to me must have thought I was mentally unbalanced, because I kept exclaiming out loud, "That's right! That's exactly our problem! That's what we need to do. Oh, yeah," and so on. I think I had highlighted practically the entire book by the time we landed!

That epiphany occurred three years ago. Shortly afterward, I contacted Dr. Borden and asked him if he would talk about his book and what he did in his judicatory with a group of district (that's what we call our middle judicatories) mission executives in Las Vegas. He graciously accepted, and, as they say, the rest is history.

I brought another staff person from my district with me to the conference, so someone else could catch the vision. Together we taped Borden's presentation and brought it back for the rest of the staff to see. They were so excited about the possibilities of truly becoming an outwardly focused district that everyone began reading Borden's book, which we discussed at our staff meetings for the next several months.

The real champion for this deep change, however, was our district president. He saw the potential of new life and vitality that this new system could bring to our judicatory, but he also realized that the American Baptist Church West was quite different from the LCMS; so he asked me to invite Borden to come to our district office. For that historic meeting we also invited key members of our board of directors and influential pastors from the district.

Equipped with the fundamentals of pastoral clusters, two-part consultations, and lay training, it was now time for us to develop a strategy that would work in our context. The first step was to select a group of congregations with pastors we thought had the capacity to become accountable leaders and thus deliver some early wins. We decided to recruit a group of twelve pastors with which to begin. We developed a Powerpoint presentation to share with them and their leaders and ten of the twelve accepted the opportunity to get into a Learning Community (our name for the pastoral cluster) and have a consultation.

A big mistake we made in selecting these initial pastors and churches was that they were spread throughout our district. In order to cover this huge geography—over eight hundred miles from end to end—we had to start four Learning Communities. It also meant that we had to have more pastors (and congregations) involved in order to achieve critical mass in each Learning Community (LC) and that we had to have a mentoring pastor for each LC. With only two pastors on our staff—the district president and myself—we were stretched very thin in the early days of our pilot project. We also ended up taking some desperate congregations that weren't the best candidates for early wins, in order to fill out all of the Learning Communities.

In retrospect, it would have been much easier to have started with a cluster of four or five pastors in one of our metro areas the first year and then expanded to another cluster in another city the next year and so on. Besides saving a huge amount of time in travel, it also would have allowed us to make fewer mistakes and to apply our new learning more gradually.

The upside of starting on a larger scale was that it forced us to learn quickly and it has allowed us to see more growth more rapidly. After two years, we now have thirty-five congregations involved in six different Learning Communities and have conducted twenty consultations. Of those thirty-five congregations, about 70 percent are growing in worship attendance. Prior to starting this revitalization process, only 20 percent of the congregations in our district were showing growth.

Another tremendous challenge that we accepted early on was to apply what we were learning in our district to our entire denomination. This truly has been the equivalent of fools rushing in where angels fear to tread! Shortly after beginning the revitalization process in our district, I was asked by our denomination to do the same thing on a national level.

The Lutheran Church—Missouri Synod has more than six thousand congregations and approximately 2.4 million members in the United States. Like many denominations, it has been declining in membership for decades. To counteract this trend and to gain a new sense of mission, the LCMS has implemented some very bold goals under the umbrella of its *Ablaze!* movement. *Ablaze!* calls for sharing the gospel of Jesus Christ with 100 million people around the world by the five hundredth anniversary of the Reformation, in 2017. This includes revitalizing two thousand churches in North America during that same time period.

For a denomination that peaked in membership in the mid-1970s and in which the vast majority of its congregations (85 percent by some estimates) are plateaued or declining in annual worship attendance, turning around fully a third of all the churches is more than a challenge. It has to be a movement directed by almighty God! Certainly, we know that "God our Savior . . . wants all [people] to be saved and to come to a knowledge of the truth" (1 Tim. 2:3-4 NIV). We also know that He has commissioned us, his followers, to "go . . . and make disciples of all [peoples]" (Matt. 28:19).

However, knowledge alone does not a movement make. If it did, our church body and our nation wouldn't be in the situation that they are in today, where we truly are surrounded by a post-church culture and many within the church are lukewarm at best. Also, if denominations could become more missional simply by legislating a new program (even if it is called a movement!) in convention, then this would have been done long ago. In fact, we have tried program after program at every level of the church with little lasting effect.

And yet, there is a genuine desire among the national and district leaders of the LCMS, and certainly among many of its congregations and pastors, to begin a new era of mission and outreach in the United States. Therefore, following the lead of Paul Borden and GHC, we formed a parachurch organization called the Transforming Churches Network, or TCN. By partnering with the LCMS, but not being intertwined with the national bureaucracy, TCN is able to stay nimble and responsive to districts and congregations and provide practical resources based on extensive research at the grassroots level.

Because the goal of revitalizing two thousand churches in the LCMS by 2017 is so large, TCN emphasizes the importance of reproducibility in its revitalization strategy. To that end, we have developed a comprehensive process designed to help congregations "regularly and consistently make new disciples and renew its members in order that they make new disciples through the power of the Holy Spirit."

The Transformation Process involves three parts:

1. *Learning Communities:* The pastor participates in a monthly cluster meeting with four to eight other pastors going through this same process. The meetings consist of training in leadership and congregational health, as well as a spiritual development component. The pastor reproduces this Learning Community in his or her own congregation among his or her own leaders.

2. *Congregational Consultation:* Following a comprehensive self-study, the congregation undergoes a weekend consultation. On this weekend, the consultation team meets with members, leaders, and staff to assess the strengths and areas of concern in the congregation's ministry. The team also makes recommendations on what changes need to take place in the church in order for it to be more missional and outward focused.

3. *Coaching:* During the year following the consultation, a trained

coach meets with the pastor on a monthly basis to help him or her grow in his leadership skills and behavior and to hold him or her accountable for the changes recommended by the consultation team. In addition, the coach meets quarterly with the congregation to communicate progress, answer questions, and hold the members accountable for their commitment to becoming a mission outpost.

For each of these major components, TCN has developed a training manual. The Learning Community manual has twenty modules that can be used over a two-year period. Each of the pastor's modules is also available in an abridged version suitable for lay leaders in a local congregation. The Consultation and Coaching manuals are only available to individuals who have been trained and certified by TCN, insuring quality control of the entire process. LCMS districts partner with TCN for the training, materials, and resources developed by TCN. In turn, the districts provide the personnel for leading the Learning Communities, assembling the consultation teams, and doing the coaching.

So far, this partnership has resulted in nearly two hundred congregations that have entered the TCN process, with thirty Learning Communities spread across the country. Of the thirty-five districts in the LCMS, twenty-four are receiving training from TCN, with some ninety consultations already conducted.

While it is too soon to tell how all of this will ultimately play out, there is certainly a great deal of excitement being generated by this process through TCN. The best way to describe this phenomenon is with the word "hope." Pastors and congregations are being given hope that the future will be better than the present, that they will not only survive but thrive, and that they can truly make a kingdom difference in their communities. Listen to the words of a typical pastor:

> We are about halfway through the plan and already I can see and sense a change. Our worship attendance is steadily increasing and we will need to expand to a third service in the new year. We are no longer financially in debt but are in fact in the black for the first time in many years (oh yeah, we're current on our mortgage payment, too!). 55 percent of first-time guests returned for two or more visits. Of the regular visitors, 50 percent of them became members. As this transformation process happens, I expect those numbers to increase.

> The new structure at our church has helped us tremendously. Now everyone knows who's in charge of what, and the lines of accountability are easy to trace. Also, the structure allows room for our church to grow; previously, ideas and planning would get bogged down in committees and meetings and nothing would get accomplished.

Of course, not everything has come up smelling like roses. Some pastors have struggled in making the kind of deep changes necessary for real church transformation to occur. For many, the biggest change is the way they use their time. Instead of spending the bulk of their time doing shepherding (taking care of their own members) and using the little time left over to minister to the community, the reverse must become the norm. Now they are expected to spend more and more of their time in personal witnessing, getting to know the needs of the community by actually being in the community, developing new leaders, and being the champion for change and a new outwardly focused vision. After spending a lifetime of ministry *to the church,* it is quite a switch for pastors to equip the church to do ministry *to its community* and then model what that looks like!

Not everyone can do it. As I mentioned earlier, we made some mistakes early on by allowing some pastors and congregations into the process that we shouldn't have. To guard against this in the future, we have developed a Pastor's Assessment Tool to gauge a pastor's readiness to enter the process. For those who fall below a certain score, we recommend that their church does not have a consultation until the pastor is given more preparatory training and demonstrates a greater degree of readiness. Also, since many congregations will continue to decline for a short period after starting the revitalization process before they start to grow, we have developed some criteria that will prevent them from falling to a level from which they cannot recover. These criteria include worship size, financial strength, no abnormal conflict, and the pastor's promise to remain with the congregation for at least five years.

One of the biggest obstacles that we have run into on the congregational side is opposition to the accountable leader model of governance. Even though most lay leaders operate under some variation of this model in their own workplaces and businesses, they struggle with the idea in church. Some think it can't be biblical, others don't want to give up the control they have in a multiple board system, and still others simply don't trust the pastor to lead them.

We have found that it is very important to carefully explain how this new system will work, demonstrate that it is biblical and within our denominational polity, and provide hands-on training for the new board, staff, and pastor. Finally, there must be clear lines of communication between all parties, and the board must actually be willing and able to hold the pastor accountable for the mission goals that have been established and enforce the agreed-upon boundary principles.

When all of these things happen, it is indeed a beautiful thing to behold. The pain that comes from fear and selfishness and apathy begins to give way to the joy that comes from life change and disciple-making and sharing Christ's sacrificial love with the world. The following story gives a small glimpse into what this transformation process can mean for a church.

Pastor Parry was tired and frustrated. He had just attended his fourth meeting in as many nights. He was working eighty-hour weeks and was just plain worn out, and for what? His leaders seemed apathetic and frustrated, the congregation was restless with his leadership, and he hardly got to see his wife and kids, except from the pulpit. In fact, his wife worked almost as many hours at the church as he did, and she wasn't even on the payroll. Pastor Parry was close to burnout and he knew it!

Of course, it hadn't always been that way. Just a couple years earlier, the church was growing, peaking at just over three hundred in worship. In his twelve years in this town of thirty-five thousand, Pastor Parry had led the small congregation from just over one hundred to its present size, steadily growing each year. Most of the newcomers were there because of his ministry. People genuinely loved him and sensed his deep commitment to reaching lost and hurting people. But it all started to unravel when the church started a new school, planted a new church across town, and experienced some internal conflict over a personnel matter. Within the last year, attendance had dropped from 320 to 235, the budget was bleeding red ink, and many people were openly disgruntled.

Pastor Parry decided something dramatic had to be done. He had heard about the revitalization process through his district leaders. One of his close friends had gone through a consultation with stellar results. With a recent inquiry to consider taking a call to a new church, he decided it was time to either move on or take the revitalization challenge. After much prayer and deliberation, he chose the latter.

Fast forward to a year later. Pastor Parry is sitting at his desk putting the final touches on his remarks for the ordination service for the new associate pastor of the church plant across town. That congregation had grown so rapidly that it already needed a second pastor. He was thankful that God had used him to plant the seeds for that new church and that he still had a close association with this daughter church and its senior pastor.

He was even more thankful that God had completely turned around his own church. His eyes fell on a news article that had recently appeared in the district's news magazine.

> On Saturday, June 20, about 50 people attended our net-fishing event. In the morning we heard an inspiring presentation about being a church with an outreach focus. In the afternoon all of the participants went out into our community to do servant evangelism events. We broke up into several groups. Some groups went prayer walking at an apartment complex with about 200 units. Other groups hung Vacation Bible School (VBS) door hangers in a neighborhood known to be full of families with children. The rest of the groups went around town handing out cold drinks on a hot day along with free t-shirts. All of the groups had great stories to tell about their interaction with individuals they met. We had a number of families send their kids to VBS.
>
> We accidentally happened upon a soapbox derby event where the crowd was extremely appreciative of the cold drinks. Kids immediately put on the t-shirts. Several people mentioned how amazing it was that we would do such a thing. Everyone who took part came away with an

excitement about being in the community and doing more such events. From the debriefing time we began to plan our next event, which is going to be a family fun party in a city park sometime in October. What a joy it was to see people so excited about getting outside the walls of the church and into the community, where we can make a greater impact on sharing the gospel through the opportunities that come with random acts of kindness.

Our VBS was held the week of July 14-18. For the second year in a row we had 120 daycampers from our YMCA. In addition we had 220 from our own church, preschool and daycampers, for a total of nearly 350 people!

On Sunday, July 20, we invited all the families to come to our regular worship service that featured the VBS program and songs. We had 75 more people than usual that day, with several families coming for the first time and who have continued coming for the past several Sundays. As part of the closing program on that Sunday, we handed out certificates to all of the VBS children that included a color picture of the children in their crew, along with their crew leader, as a reminder of the wonderful time they had at VBS.

Having gone through the revitalization process, our congregation not only allowed the second service to be used in this way, but they actually encouraged it. We had more volunteers involved than in previous years and everyone was excited about doing it and trusting God to work through it. What a difference from past years when volunteers were sometimes hard to find.

What a difference, indeed, Pastor Parry thought. In one year, worship attendance had increased back to 320, the church budget was in the black, there was a renewed sense of joy on Sunday morning, and a strong sense of unity and love among the members and staff. But the best thing was that lives were being changed among both the members and the many new people to whom the church was reaching out.

As he laid down his pen, Pastor Parry thought, "If you had told me a year ago that this is where we would be today, I would have had my doubts. How thankful I am that God has bigger plans than I do and that He continues to bless us in ways that we hadn't dreamed of yet. Now I can't wait to see how things will change and grow by this time next year!"

With that prayer in his heart, he walked out of his office into a bright new tomorrow.

Testimony 2: The Salvation Army, Australia Southern Territory

Introduction

Kelvin Merrett[2] serves as the Director of the Growing Healthy Corps (GHC) Network for The Salvation Army's Australia Southern Territory. He is responsible for a pilot scheme that sees forty-five Salvation Corps (churches), with their officers (pastors) being part of the GHC Network. The Network spreads throughout the eight divisions of the Territory.

He came into his role as director after eighteen months in the position of Corps Programme Secretary (having responsibility for the oversight of Corps programs). "The territory was not in the best shape," says Kelvin. "Over the previous ten years the total Sunday morning attendances (our main time for people attending church) had dropped 2 percent every year. That was a 20 percent decline over ten years; it was clearly time to change our way of thinking and our methodology of doing church! We are now coming to the end of our third year of the pilot and we have seen some great results."

Kelvin recently analyzed the Corps that had been in the pilot for two years or more. At the commencement of the pilot these Corps had a decline in attendance of 3 percent. These same Corps now have a combined growth in attendance of 3 percent. That's a 6 percent turnaround in just under three years!

The Salvation Army's journey to this point has not been a quick one! There was a three-year journey before the network was launched. The initial introduction of Paul Borden to the Territory was made by John Vale (a man passionate to see growth happening), who invited Paul to make a presentation to the senior leadership team (cabinet). This then led to the first of five annual "Reversing the Decline" Conferences. Kelvin Merrett in his role as Corps Programme Secretary was given responsibility to explore Borden's methods further. The big question was whether the GHC concepts could be used in Australia. What were the cultural differences? What would be the point of adopting yet another programme from America?

Kelvin, with a team of three others, spent a week with Paul in Northern California. There were three key discoveries.

The clusters that were operating provided a great environment for pastors to learn and develop as leaders. It was great to see how these pastors "championed" each other. They had an environment where they could learn and share their concerns in a safe environment.

These pastors, while becoming effective leaders that were growing their local churches, were "normal" people. They were not "super pastors" but men and women who could be officers back in Australia. This was an important discovery for the Australian team. Men and women called by God and equipped for leadership were making a difference. They were growing their churches; they were influencing their communities.

The clusters were something that would translate to Australia and our culture. The clusters would fit the culture of Australia.

While Kelvin and his team had decided that the cluster concept and a GHC Network would work in Australia, there needed to be a strategy as to how to introduce this into The Salvation Army. The Salvos structure is based on a military command structure. There are three levels of command: the senior leadership of the Army with a Cabinet, headed by a Territorial Commander; a Divisional Leadership (Bishop) leading a Division; and the local Corps Leadership, led by the Corps Officers. The Network needed to cross over traditional boundaries. Divisional Leaders needed to put the need of the territory first.

A series of workshops were held with the territorial and divisional leaders, with Paul invited to tell the story of the American Baptist Church of the West and present the principles of the GHC

Network. This allowed for the leaders of The Salvation Army to have a full understanding of the process and also allowed for buy-in. It was not an easy decision for the senior leadership to make.

Once the decision was made to proceed with the pilot at this level, further workshops were held, such as the consultation training, so there was transparency in the process and senior leadership knew exactly what was happening. By this time a second "Reversing the Decline" conference was held and initial selections for cluster membership were made from officers who had attended these conferences. A decision was also made that allowed Kelvin Merrett to be released from other responsibilities so he could drive the rollout of the Network.

It was decided that suitable Corps matched with suitable officers would be the way to go. A cluster group of four to five Corps would be set up in every division. Corps leadership teams themselves would not be consulted. The rationale for the latter decision was the thinking that if the Corps officers were on board they then had one to three years to prepare the Corps for a consultation/intervention. This has not proved to be a negative move.

An important step for The Salvation Army was to agree for a clause to be placed in the covenant that officers would remain in their appointments for an additional five years and the Army would allow them to stay. This was an important win for a movement that has an appointment system for its officers. Generally, the establishment of clusters has worked well. In some cases we deliberately selected Corps where we knew there would be an intervention required but had confidence in the officers to give the leadership (with the necessary support and training).

The clusters are being greatly valued by the officers attending. Non-Salvation Army facilitators have been engaged who have grown their own congregations. This has been an important principle. Officers have greatly benefited from the practical lessons learned from practitioners. Agreement was given to engaging non-salvos as facilitators because it was felt to be an important principle that facilitators should be experienced and successful leaders of growing their own congregations and had kingdom values. This was a bold step for The Salvation Army. This does not mean The

Salvation Army does not have competent officers—it reflects an appointment system where competent officers have traditionally been "promoted" to larger Corps or other leadership positions.

Opportunity in clusters for officers to learn about principles of church health and leadership in the morning, followed by spiritual discoveries in the afternoon, has worked well. It has been a challenge for some officers to keep up with the reading requirements, but this is part of the expectations. The coaching of officers (another requirement is that all officers have a coach) is proving to be valuable, although some officers, particularly those living in remote locations, have difficulty in finding suitable coaches. The coaches are responsible for holding their officer accountable for the personal and appointment goals being set.

For a structure as tightly controlled as The Salvation Army, the time spent in developing the network with the senior leadership was vital. It allowed the senior leaders to own the strategy. The time frame has also been valuable in "selling" the Network to Corps. Many of the lay leaders of congregations were skeptical about another new program. To be able to outline the process has been valuable—it has also allowed The Salvation Army to emphasise that the GHC Network is a process and not a program. It is the beginning of systemic change.

The full impact of consultations was not realized when the Network was commenced. These are proving to be vital to the process. While some Corps Officers have been reluctant to take them up—wanting to spend more time getting their Corps ready—the reality is that for some the consultation is an intervention and Corps will never be "ready." The consultations have provided excellent opportunity to introduce needed change into the life of Corps. On most occasions there are no real surprises for the Corps officers. What they now have is permission to introduce the needed change. The GHC Network undertakes to continue to support the Corps after the consultation. It is reassuring for the Corps to know they will have ongoing support.

The key prescriptions that have continued to arise from most consultations are:

- *The need for a fresh vision to commence a new life cycle.* The life-cycle concepts are important, as they have become the cornerstone for all teaching, particularly for the lay leadership of Corps. It gives permission to try new initiatives but in a framework of support and direction.

- *The need to repent for not making disciples.* The importance of becoming outward focused; of realising again what the mission of The Salvation Army is all about, is happening through the days of prayer.

- *The need for a functional leadership structure to enable growth to take place.* The need for a new leadership structure in Corps is putting into place the first steps of needed systemic change in The Salvation Army.

One of the ongoing concerns is the training of future consultants. The Australian culture has what is called the "tall-poppy" syndrome. (People of genuine merit are criticised or resented because their talents or achievements elevate them above or distinguish them from their peers.) This means that local consultants will be well received—as long as there is someone of distinction working alongside them. Also, in the history of The Salvation Army in the Southern Territory, there are not many locals who have grown their own Corps and have the needed credibility. In time officers who have been part of a successful consultation will become lead consultants. As part of the training, officers are assisting in consultations (going in as part of the consultation team). In the future it is planned that consultations will be led by a small consultation team (three to four), with one of these officers as the lead consultant. This will also be an ongoing framework for training new consultants.

The principles that are being taught at cluster meetings and during consultations are being reinforced at the Layered Learning events. How these are held varies from cluster to cluster. Examples include John Kaiser speaking on the leadership structure of churches; Paul Borden speaking on the life cycle; and local facilitators leading events that are relevant to the local needs. The Layered Learning events are also a great place for momentum to build. Lay leaders become energized when they share with other leaders. It is great to hear stories of lay leaders from one Corps helping out another Corps by sharing their own experiences in the process.

The introduction of Super Clusters has added another important dynamic to the leadership training for Corps officers. These have provided great momentum and energy by bringing together ninety plus officers for training every year. Divisional leaders are always invited, so they can remain on the same page as their Corps officers. It has been encouraging to see divisional leaders attending the Super Clusters, and it is always appreciated by the Corps officers.

The momentum of the GHC Network continues to grow. There have now been five Growing Healthy Corps Conferences (the name was changed from Reversing the Decline to give a positive emphasis). This means that nearly every Corps officer in the Southern Territory has had exposure to the basic principles of GHC.

As the Network has continued to be developed, there has been a growing demand from officers to join. This is a positive challenge as The Salvation Army keeps up with the current demands of the pilot.

Kelvin Merrett's Story

Whitehall Corps is located in a small rural town of seven thousand people in Victoria. The town's people do not have a positive outlook and the town's economy is in recession. The Corps officers had earlier cast a vision which had seen this Corps move to becoming outward focused. New people had commenced attending and making Whitehall their spiritual home.

Before having a consultation, the officers had been to a Growing Healthy Corps conference with Paul Borden and had been inspired to change their leadership style and give intentional leadership that would lead to growth. The GHC principles and methodology gave them a framework to date this. They were further supported by the GHC Clusters, under the leadership of an experienced facilitator. At the time of the consultation the Corps had plateaued, but its strengths included an outward-focused congregation (evangelism was a strength) and committed people giving good leadership to children's ministries.

The consultation team identified the following five concerns:

1. *Life Cycle:* The Corps is past the peak of its current life cycle. There is no vision in place for the next five years. The lack of vision if not addressed will cause the Corps to move quickly downwards in its life cycle.

2. *No Process for Discipleship:* There is no process in place to help new Christians become mature, reproducing disciples. The result is a myriad of activities that produce little spiritual development in people.

3. *Stalled Growth.* The Corps has plateaued in its numerical growth. It has also plateaued in evangelism growth.

4. *Leadership Development:* The Corps lacks leaders. Many of the leaders in place have not been equipped to oversee their ministry responsibilities.

5. *Assimilation:* There is no assimilation process in place to help new disciples become mobilized for ministry.

The prescriptions of the weekend addressed the concerns. While there was general acceptance, not all of the leadership team were on board. Change meant the empowering of more leaders—with former leaders not having the same level of influence they had previously experienced.

The consultation again highlighted the need for an up-to-date vision for the Corps. Once the goals of the previous vision had been realized, growth had stopped, and people quickly became comfortable. There was a pressure to consolidate and make good what had happened, rather than push into the future with a new vision. The consultation's prescriptions gave license to the Corps officers to revision the Corps, giving it fresh life.

There was a need for a discipleship process to be implemented. No process was in place to help new Christians become mature, reproducing disciples, resulting in a myriad of activities that produced little spiritual development in people. The consultation made discipleship training a priority, an issue that needed to be attended to.

One of the reasons the Corps had stalled in its growth was because it had run out of room. So it was prescribed that the Corps would move into multiple services; each service tailored for the people it wanted to reach. Seating needed to be changed to accommodate the changing needs of the congregations.

The Corps officers needed to be up-skilled. While they were great officers, they needed to know what was required next of them—to take the Corps onto the next level.

A final step was the introduction of an assimilation program.

The strength of the consultations is that it narrows the focus for the Corps and provides distinct courses of action that need to be implemented—a quick means that ensures action steps can be quickly implemented. (This Corps had already introduced a staff-led leadership model, part of the GHC principles.)

While there will always be friction and resistance, the GHC Network, with its cluster meetings and other resources, provides a framework that gives Corps officers the confidence to step out and move on to the next level of leadership needed. After only a few months the Corps officers were able to report:

> We have got all of our new services up and running and we have seen some great results. In the 4 weeks since we have started the new services we have had 20 new people through our doors—and 5 people have been saved. We had 80 people at our two new Friday services.

The consultations are the line-in-the-sand events that Corps need to have. They provide:

- the first steps that need to be taken;
- an opportunity for everyone to be on the same page;
- an opportunity for Corps to turn around and grow.

Testimony 3: Florida Church of God Ministries
By Dr. Greg Wiens[3]

Florida Church of God Ministries is part of a larger movement called the Church of God, Anderson, IN, which distinguishes us from the other fifty or so denominations that have Church of God in their name. We began in the 1880s as a reaction to strong denominationalism, and our founders had a strong passion for holiness. In the United States, we are broken up into about thirty-eight different regions or judicatories; I oversee the state of Florida. Traditionally, my position has been more administrative, with responsibilities such as handling paperwork of transfers, coordinating church planting, and attempting to mediate conflict within churches. However, in the years prior to my taking this position, the state desired more of a leader position and rewrote the job description to reflect this. My predecessor was a wonderfully gifted leader and inspired great trust in the position, which clearly positioned me to make significant changes.

From 1962 to 2002 our national movement lost a net of about 60 churches (approximately 2,560 down to 2,500), while the number of churches specifically in Florida increased by about 54 churches (60 churches to 114 churches). So as a judicatory we were growing in our number of churches and actually our *average* church attendance had dramatically increased during this same period (from about 66 to 113). In 2002, however, I knew most of our churches were *not* growing. So I analyzed the attendance figures and found that 90 percent of our congregations were plateaued, declining, or closing for the previous five years (see table #1).

Beginning in 1999, I had utilized Natural Church Development (NCD) and the commensurate coaching to turn around some of our plateaued churches. We consulted with about twenty churches over the next several years and spent countless hours in coaching implementation teams through their strategies to deal with their minimum factors. We saw an initial surge of growth as the minimum factors were addressed. However, after several years I noticed that systemic issues began to impede growth and health. These issues often concerned power structures, flawed DNA, inadequate pastoral leadership, and sin. In our tradition, I have little ecclesial authority (remember, we were born out of a reaction to strong denominationalism). I can only deal with issues in churches when invited to do so, or if there has been a clear violation of our credentialing process (of pastors or churches). So when we would begin to deal with some of these deep systemic issues, the church or leadership would tell me they were done with the process. In other words, I could help the church or leadership deal with issues until they got to a point they no longer wanted me to deal with a really painful issue or an underlying issue, then I was done.

This happened repeatedly, and finally, in frustration, I began to seek and pray for a different approach. Through a Lilly grant from our national offices, we received funds to begin leadership training clusters for our pastors. We sought out the best training and trainers from around the nation to speak into the pastors' lives. We used these monthly cluster meetings to encourage and train our pastors in leading healthy, outward-focused churches. Our pastors got excited about leading missional churches but, unfortunately, many of the churches were not excited about some of the necessary changes to become outward focused. As a result, some of the pastors in our clusters were leaving their churches. We were coaching the pastors to be healthy, outward focused leaders, but then they went back into unhealthy churches (systems)—similar to drying out an alcoholic and then sending them back into a dysfunctional system. If you train a pastor to become outward focused, you must alter the system to accommodate this change. But we were not changing the systems of churches.

Thus, we tried to develop an in-depth process that would look at the systemic issues and gain the trust of the leadership and church. We experimented with this process in several churches, going through a three-month period of consulting, training, and education. But, in the end, we still lacked the authority to deal with the real issues. It was then I read Paul Borden's book, *Hit the Bullseye.*

Obviously, we had a number of the pieces in place, but we lacked a coherent system to tie together what we were learning *and* the authority to deal with the issues in churches that were really keeping them unhealthy. Paul's concept of consultations and covenants was the answer. The consultation was a process that would allow the church to own their dysfunctional systems and to agree to our help. We would give them all of the data possible to show them why and where they needed help. Because of our polity, I felt it was best to add an additional step beyond what Paul was using in his process.

During the consultation process, we spent time in prayer, preparation, and collecting information, then presented our recommendations to the congregation and leadership. At this point, we did not want to go any further if the church was not in support of the recommendations. We asked that the congregation spend two weeks praying about these recommendations before they voted. Only after a positive vote (as determined by what their by-laws required for a by-laws change) would we then write up a covenant to implement these recommendations. The covenant spells out in detail who will do what, by when, and how it will be paid for. This covenant also gives authority to the judicatory to implement the necessary changes. It does not give the judicatory authority to take over the church—only to make the changes necessary to see health established in the church. This means different things in different church contexts. Every covenant is unique.

This covenant is brought before the congregation and we ask the congregation to spend another several weeks asking questions and praying over this document before a second vote is taken. If there is a positive vote on the covenant as well (by the same percentage as previously determined by the by-laws), we then have church leaders, witnesses, and judicatory leaders sign the covenant. This process allows us to work with a congregation for usually two months while they fill out the self-study, and another six weeks through the consultation, recommendations, and covenant phase. By this time, we have been with the congregation and leadership for three to four months. There has been time for trust to be established and the covenant gives the judicatory the authority to deal with issues that are impeding health for a period of three years.

As we have implemented and modified this process, we have found many churches willing to go through the process. During the past four years we have taken twenty churches through it. We still have a list of churches asking for our help because of the results we have seen these past four to five years. In 2000, only 10 percent of our churches were growing (compared to the previous five years); last year that figure rose to 25 percent.

Because of our polity and heritage, we continually have to fight the perception that we are "taking over churches." We are passionate about seeing churches become healthy and transform their communities through the power and presence of the living Christ. We see this demonstrated through multiplying converts, disciples, leaders, and congregations. In coming alongside of churches, often we need to make changes that can be painful to certain segments of the church. Through the covenant we have the authority to make such changes, especially when it is painful and the patient resists. For three years our involvement is invasive, but we do not want to be involved in the life of healthy, growing churches. Our goal is to see them become healthy and growing, then get out of their way. We want to serve them as they change the spiritual landscape in their community.

Recently I received a call from one of our national denominational executives asking me if I knew there was a group in Florida that was taking over churches, removing Church of God from their names, replacing leadership, and taking ownership of their buildings. I laughed as I told him that yes, I was aware of the group, and it was *us!* I quickly corrected him by telling him we haven't changed any names and we surely haven't taken control or ownership of facilities (unless a church has closed). But this goes to show the degree of fear of such "takeover" within our movement.

Being aware of this fear five years ago, I sponsored a lunch for pastors of twenty of our largest churches before I did anything. I sent them a copy of the book *Hit the Bullseye* and asked them to read it. During this meeting I explained my frustrations and desires for our movement. I asked them to support me during the critical transition period that would be required for these significant changes within the judicatory. I felt because of their size they would understand the need or challenges required to transition our model from that of a chaplaincy to a missional mindset. I received overwhelming support from those who attended.

Not only was it critical that we enlist the larger-church pastors, I also knew that without prayer our efforts would be futile. This is truly a spiritual battle and we are not battling against flesh and blood. So I enlisted one spiritual prayer warrior I knew in the state. She was eighty years old and used a wheelchair. We met every week personally and communicated constantly through e-mail for the next five years for prayer. Before and during each consultation she was on her knees, lifting us before our Lord. She died (should I say, graduated) this past year and the world will never know the battles that were won on her knees before we experienced them as a reality.

We were converting our judicatory from a hospice chaplaincy to a missional-focused, aggressive wellness-training program. I fired my staff in an attempt to align all of our resources toward a missional focus. Some of the staff were "rehired" under new titles, but the way we did the ministry within the judicatory took a major shift. Some of the fired staff still haven't forgiven me. I wrote to all of our pastors explaining what the changes would look like and offered to meet with them to answer questions. We offered our services for consultation freely to any church that desired them. I would fund the entire cost of a consultation out of my judicatory budget ($5,000-$12,000 apiece).

We wrote completely new by-laws for the Florida Church of God Ministries, which allowed us to operate under an Accountable Leadership Model (see John Kaiser's book entitled *Winning on Purpose*). This provided me the accountability to focus on mission while keeping moral and financial expectations in place. Every year the staff and I set missional goals, which are negotiated and agreed upon by the elders. The model clearly provides me the freedom to lead the judicatory and our elders to govern, which is to ensure I stay within agreed-upon boundaries.

One of the biggest challenges to making these changes came from within me. I had to learn to lead differently. I had to learn to lead without the respect of some of national stature in our movement. I had to learn to focus on Florida and not anywhere else. I resigned all of my positions of influence outside of Florida Church of God Ministries. This was more difficult than I anticipated. I didn't realize how much of my ego needs were being met by some of these "perks." I agree with Robert Quinn (*Deep Change*) when he says most organizations fail to make systemic change because their leader is not willing to make the commensurate changes *within* himself or herself.

There have been numerous negative reactions about the way we have been doing ministry these past five years. Some pastors have complained that they would like to have more direction into how I spend my time or would like simply to spend more time with me (read chaplain). At one point a pastor who had relocated to the state literally accused me of some sort of moral failure for the way a state meeting was run (we don't spend hours discussing budgets, etc.). This is why we have elders. Our elders handle those kinds of criticism, which is part of governance.

I have received criticism from laypeople who no longer feel comfortable because their church is growing through reaching lost people and making disciples. They liked it when it was like a family and they don't like "those" kinds of people. We have been ostracized from national initiatives because we don't play by their rules in propagating longstanding ministries.

Everything we do at the judicatory level is measured by how it serves the local church to become healthy in its pursuit of transforming its community. I believe Florida Church of God Ministries only exist to build healthy churches that are multiplying converts, disciples, leaders, and churches. We do not exist to promote a national movement or ourselves. The local church is the reason we exist.

We have had to face a number of problems as we endeavored to make these changes at the judicatory level. The first was that we did not have the funds to come in and finance a turnaround of very many churches. So we were creative in using funds from a procured line of credit on the facilities of the church. Ironically, most of the churches that were plateaued, declining, or closing were fairly well off financially. They had been built by the Builders generation and, for the most part, their facilities were paid for and they had money in a variety of "dedicated" or "rainy day" accounts. We simply needed to tap into those cherished resources for outward-focused ministry in the present. Often we have to write into the covenant that we can access these funds for turnaround endeavors.

Even with this we found ourselves very short of cash flow. At one point in the ministry, I had to decide whether I would let one of my staff go or not support a pastor's salary for one of our covenant churches. The decision was easy, yet difficult. I let my staff member go, and we still have not been able to rehire someone for this position. My experience has taught me that no judicatory turnaround will occur without significant pain to the leader and the organization.

We quickly learned that we did not have the networks or the finances to bring in high-powered pastors with proven track records to turn churches around. We have had to remediate more pastors as well as use unproven candidates whom we could train. We have had to develop a training module for many of our expected outcomes for healthy churches. We had to develop Bootcamp, which is intensive and short (one week long), to train and assess these potential pastors. We learned the hard way that we cannot assume a pastor understands the difference between healthy transition and overnight change.

Another lesson we learned on the way was that we did not have the personnel resources and experience that Paul Borden had in his judicatory. In spite of making some strategic staff hires, we still lacked the punch that Paul and his staff were able to coalesce. So we adapted the approach to be much more team oriented. Everything we do is based upon having a team of coaches (some paid, but mostly unpaid) fulfill the consultation ministry expectations. Our Consultation Team is comprised of twelve coaches. Most of them are pastors in growing churches within our state. A number have experienced a consultation themselves and have learned first-hand what it takes to turn a church around.

The entire consultation team reviews each consultation self-study that is completed by a local church. We then select a small subset of the coaches (three to five, depending on the size of the church) to participate in the consultation weekend. After the recommendation and covenant stages are complete, we then assign a lead coach to coach the pastor of that church monthly for the life of the covenant (three years). This lead coach has the entire consultation coaching team at his or her disposal for assistance and accountability.

In addition to the coaching the pastor of the covenant church receives from the lead coach, the pastor is also expected to be part of a coaching cluster. These are the groups that we have had functioning before we developed consultations. However, in order to get into a coaching cluster now, your church has to commit to going through a consultation within the next eighteen months. Three to four times a year, we bring in outside resources such as authors and pastors to train these pastors. All of the clusters will meet together for this time with the outside resource person. These "superclusters" are times for pastors of covenant churches to bring their staff and leaders to a training event.

In Florida Church of God Ministries, we have also used these resource people to offer a training time for all of the pastors and leaders in the state. I am convinced this has raised the level of awareness to a heightened state. In other words, as all pastors and leaders are exposed to these kinds of missional-minded thinkers and communicators, they too begin to change their expectations of what a healthy church should look like. These events continue to open doors into churches for consultations.

Now there clearly is an expectation in Florida Church of God Ministries that we exist to build healthy churches. Many of our churches now expect to grow through seeing people come to Christ and then making disciples. Most of our churches are no longer content with remaining as a close, loving family. This is borne out in our numbers. Ironically, during the decade of most rapid population growth in Florida, Florida Church of God Ministries did not grow rapidly. From 1995 to 2000, our churches lost 1.3 percent in attendance. However, during the last five years, we have grown by 12.4 percent! From 1995 to 2000, only 10 percent of our churches sustained at least a 2 percent growth for the five years. From 2003 to 2008, 25 percent of our churches have sustained that growth (see Table 1).

In 1998, 67 percent of our churches were below one hundred in attendance. In 2008, that figure is 52 percent (see Table 2). Our churches are not only becoming bigger, they are becoming healthier. This has not been easy, but it has been effective.

In closing, I just received an e-mail from one of our covenant pastors. He said they had almost 140 in service last week, during the middle of the summer! He is elated, and you may not think this is much to celebrate about, but let me briefly describe the church.

This church did not really care for Florida Church of God Ministries for a number of reasons. They were a church that had struggled from time to time and continued to go from one pastor to another. Each time, they ended up with fewer people than before. First, I needed to go to the church and apologize for our share of the misunderstandings over the years. Next, they asked us to help them find their next pastor. I told them we first needed to do a consultation to determine the right kind of pastor, to which they agreed. One of the recommendations included us selecting the next pastor, which is not in keeping with our tradition. But they agreed and passed the covenant.

The search process took over a year to find a pastor who culturally fit the area and had a proven history of being outward-focused. During this year we implemented an Accountable Leadership Model in the church. I personally was the coach during this time and I met with their leadership at least monthly. We went through a variety of training modules; teaching them what a healthy church valued and how it operated. We rewrote their bylaws and had a transition pastor model what being an outward-focused church looked like. Finally, we found a pastor with a Methodist background from an Internet inquiry. We assessed him and we hired him. There were 33 people in the church at that point.

The week he arrived he made radical changes. Unfortunately, most of the people left over the next few months, and the finances became desperately low. A line of credit was taken out on the facility and a part-time worship leader was hired. A significant Easter outreach was planned and executed, paid for by the judicatory. This outreach included a free fair for children with big inflatables among other initiatives. Several hundred local residents came to the event. The judicatory also underwrote some of the salary for the pastor and worship leader.

Now, a little over a year after the pastor came, I have received this e-mail about having 136 in attendance with no special event, just a normal summer Sunday in Florida. Only two of the original people (the original chairman of the leadership board and his wife) are still attending. Those who left were valuable to the kingdom of God (most of them are over the age of 70). Unfortunately, they simply could not make the shift to being missionaries to reach younger people. They have baptized twenty-four people this past year, and there are plenty of tattoos and piercings on their bodies. This is what we call Kingdom expansion. They are transforming their community for Christ. That is why we exist.

Florida Church of God Ministries: Table 1

Year	Number of attendees	Five-year growth[1]	Number of churches	Average attendance	Percentage of churches not growing[2]	Percentage of churches growing[3]
2000	12,644	-1.3%	110	114.9	90%	10%
2002	12,948	7.6%	114	113.6	86%	14%
2008	14,553	12.4%	111	131.1	75%	25%

[1] Percentage of change of the state Sunday a.m. attendance over the previous five years
[2] Plateaued, declining, or closed over the last five years
[3] Growing at least 2 percent per year for the last five years

Florida Church of God Ministries: Table 2

Church size	1998	2008
Churches of fewer than 100	67%	52%
Churches 100-199	20%	26%
Churches 200-299	5%	10%
Churches 300+	8%	11%
Since 2000, 25 churches have closed, 26 churches have been planted.		

Florida Church of God Ministries: Table 3

State of Florida figures on population and growth				
Year	1980	1990	2000	2007
Population	9,746,961	12,937,926	15,982,378	18,680,367
Rate of growth per decade		32.7%	23.5%	16.9%	

Testimony 4: Trinity Fellowship Association of Churches
By Marty Rowley[4] and Royce Gooch[5]

TFAC[6] is an association of independent, charismatic churches, started in 1994, as an outreach ministry of Trinity Fellowship Church of Amarillo, Texas, to be a place of connection, fellowship, and resourcing for independent charismatic churches in a five-state region around Amarillo. Our mission is "to advance God's Kingdom by partnering with and planting healthy, growing, reproducing ministries in the five-state region surrounding Amarillo, Texas."

Our Story

In 2005, after several years of operation, Marty Rowley, the president of Trinity Fellowship Association of Churches (TFAC), recognized that our organization of approximately thirty churches was not impacting the kingdom of God in our five-state region in the way that we should be. Out of our thirty churches, we could only count about three that we could consider growing churches. The rest were either on a plateau or were slowly declining. While the pastors in these churches were totally committed to faithfully fulfilling the ministry that God had placed them into and were ministering to the people of their congregations, discouragement was evident in their faces as they would come together for our meetings with them. They wanted God to use them to reach new disciples for Jesus Christ, but they were finding that the way to do so was beyond their reach. It was against this backdrop that we began searching for a way to bring new levels of health to these existing congregations so that our collective desire to impact the kingdom of God could be more fully realized. About that time, Dr. Paul Borden was in the process of writing the book *Hit the Bullseye*. One of our staff members had served under Dr. Borden at an earlier time in their ministries, and Dr. Borden had been sending him copies of the chapters of the book as they were being written. As we reviewed these chapters, we began to think that Dr. Borden's approach might be useful to us in helping the churches that were coming to us for guidance and resources.

In 2006, we launched what we termed the "TFAC Church Health Initiative." We began by forming our first Coaching Group (our terminology for the cluster meetings). This group was to be a pilot group of seven of our churches, brought together to test Dr. Borden's process in our "church culture." Given the fact that Dr. Borden's process was initially developed in a Baptist environment, we were a little unsure as to how some of the elements of the process would work where the churches were governed differently. In our association, each congregation is governed by a group of elders and there is very little in the way of congregational votes. While the elders in our churches are spiritual leaders in the church, their function, as elders, is more like a corporate board of directors than a "normal" church board. These elders provide spiritual oversight to the ministries of the churches but have no direct staff oversight unless that is specifically delegated to them by the whole elder board. In addition, they provide governmental oversight to the senior pastor of the church. In our model of governance, the senior pastor articulates the vision for the congregation and the elders are charged with clarifying and ratifying that vision. When that is done, the day-to-day operation of the church becomes the responsibility of the senior pastor and his staff. There was also the issue of our part of the country being deep in the "Bible Belt" of the United States.

It appeared that Dr. Borden's strategy was developed in a part of the country in which people will confess to being more "pagan" than they will in our part of the country. Here in Amarillo, Texas, most people will describe themselves as "Christian" even if they have not had a recent experience with Jesus Christ. The religious environment is such that our population may even be considered somewhat "inoculated" against the gospel of Jesus Christ. This geographical difference was an area that we wanted to investigate as we tested this strategy here.

As we began implementing this strategy, we started with having our initial coaching group meet once a month here in our facilities in Amarillo. The seven pastors and five of our TFAC staff members met to discuss whatever book we had been assigned to read that month and to go through a teaching on church health, church life cycles, leadership and the like, and to find out how each church was doing in response to what we were learning in the group. As we went through the books and the teachings, we attempted to find ways to implement what we were learning at each of the churches, or to find ways to help the elders, staff, and congregation more fully understand what we were learning and why it was important. There were a couple of things that were a little difficult for us. One was a particular characteristic of members of independent, charismatic churches that often reveals itself as an unhealthy focus on "what's in it for me?" Actually, that may often be a characteristic of American Christians as a whole. Another one of the more difficult things we faced was that some of the leaders of our churches were not used to having outside input. Accordingly, they sometimes found it difficult to accept our attempts to effect some kind of transformation. Both of these things were apparent, at times, during the whole process of this pilot group and presented a unique challenge for our initiative. Overall, one of the best outcomes of the coaching groups has been that the relationship between the pastors has risen to a level that we've always wanted to see but have had difficulty in achieving. The intimacy of the coaching groups has radically improved our efforts to provide a relational connection for these pastors.

In an effort to provide an overview of the things the pastors were learning in the coaching group, we hosted several Lay Training events here in Amarillo and invited all the elders, staff, and congregations of the TFAC-affiliated churches to these events. We video-recorded these events so that we could use them to impart the information to those churches who would be involved after the pilot group and to churches in the pilot group whose congregations could not attend the training events. As we have moved beyond the pilot stage, we now send these recorded events to the churches involved in the process and we make a TFAC staff member available to emcee the training event so that someone is available to answer questions from the congregation members.

One of the most valuable aspects of our initiative was our Church Health Consultations. We held these individual consultation weekends in each of the seven churches. This was a very effective process for providing specific recommendations for improvement in each of these churches. These consultations have provided initial targets for things to be done in an effort to turn the focus of the individual churches outward toward the people of the community and the needs of the community. During these consultations we were able to uncover several issues in various churches that had the potential to cause major division in the congregation or to result in leadership failures among the current church leadership. While these issues were not communicated directly to the congregation in the form of a report, we were able to deal effectively with the issues and help resolve them before more damage was done. Some of the consultations resulted in the pastor seeking counseling for personal issues, some in the recommendation of a sabbatical for the senior pastor and his wife, and in some cases, the consultation resulted in some staff members leaving because they couldn't get on board with the idea of being outwardly focused. While these issues were challenging, the consultation resulted in these seven churches having clearer and more defined visions for their futures and their pastors and staff being better trained to carry that vision forward in each instance.

After the pilot group finished the initial twelve-month process, we were so encouraged by the results that we decided to roll out the same series of teachings and books to the rest of our membership. We elected to extend the initial process to sixteen months so that the study load was lessened. We also decided the process was so important that any church that wanted to be a part of our membership needed to be a part of the process. It was here that we ran into our first really major snag. For whatever reason, maybe our strong enthusiasm over the process and pressure to have all our members participate, maybe the perceived threat of increased accountability, or some other reason, we're not totally sure, we began to have some of our churches balk at going through the process. Eventually, about five of our original thirty churches left the association over this change of emphasis. A common phrase that we heard was, "we believe God is taking us another direction." While it was a little discouraging to us, we decided that we had to continue pursuing the direction that we were taking because we believed that God had brought us to this place and was allowing us to see something that could help us achieve the mission of expanding the Kingdom in our five-state region.

We have completed, or nearly completed, what we would call Phase II of our implementation of this strategy of transformation. This phase involved integrating all of our remaining members into the process. We continue to rely heavily on the coaching groups and the consultations as primary tools. As we communicate the need to cast vision repetitively, our pastors seem to be good at bringing the congregation along in their understanding of why their particular church can benefit from participating in this strategy.

Our congregations seem to be catching on to the need to be outwardly focused, and many exciting things are occurring because our churches are making specific efforts to connect with and benefit the communities that they serve. In our area, which is predominately rural, each of our churches really serves a community that is larger than the town where they are located, so the idea of serving their community takes on a little different look than it would in a large city or urban area.

The coaching groups have become places where our pastors have the freedom to speak about the issues that they are facing and be able to trust the confidentiality of the group. These groups have become sanctuaries for these pastors and we often hear how they look forward to coming to their monthly coaching group.

We have completed almost all the consultations, so that all our churches have had an on-site visit from a Church Consultation team. Even though the idea can be a little intimidating, we have found that most of our pastors and congregations have eventually appreciated the results of the consultations. This appreciation comes especially after they figure out that we're really trying to help them do the ministry they've been called to in a more effective way and not trying to publicly point out all their faults.

As we continue implementing this strategy, we are beginning to develop our own teaching material and book lists. We are also making every effort to connect our members to the coaching groups and to emphasize the importance of this involvement for each of the churches. We are finding that we are quickly coming to a point where the recommendations from the first round of consultations are either being totally completed or they are becoming less relevant because of changed circumstances in a particular congregation. We are now making plans to begin a second round of consultations within our existing coaching groups to address these new situations.

We are still facing the difficulty of the geographical separation between our churches in bringing our pastors together for these meetings, and we anticipate that these separation distances and the current high price of transportation will continue to be issues.

One issue we are recognizing now is that as we continue to expand our association of churches, we will have a need to bring the new members up to speed on the initial information related to leadership, church health, and church life cycles. The fact that many of our new members may be in geographical areas where we don't have enough members to form a coaching group adds to the difficulty of bringing these "new member" groups together. We are now beginning to evaluate alternative ways of holding coaching group meetings that would utilize technology solutions in lieu of travel for the meetings. While face-to-face meetings are more desirable, we hope that technology solutions will help when those single-site meetings are not possible.

As a result of us implementing this strategy of transformation, we are beginning to see a difference in the pastors and the congregations of our association. The pastors have a closer relationship with each other than ever before. Our churches and the leaders of these churches are seeing the benefit of being outwardly focused in the pursuit of obedience to the Great Commission. Our communities are seeing the love of Christ portrayed in the tangible acts of the leaders and members of the churches. Many of our churches are now becoming churches that are seen as essential parts of their communities, givers to the community and not takers. Many of our churches are now beginning to grow again, due to their interaction with the community. We have noticed that sometimes a church that begins to shift their focus outward will initially decline in attendance as those who say "what's in it for me?" begin to leave for other churches. We've had several of those situations develop, but those churches are still healthier today than they have been in the past. We trust that as these churches continue to pursue their focus on making disciples, growth will come as new disciples of Jesus Christ are born into the family of God.

Our experiment with this strategy has been tremendously successful and we are continuing to use this approach as we begin to expand our association with new members. We believe that of the numerous changes that our association has experienced in the last several years, this approach to our ministry has been the best thing we've ever offered our members.

Turnaround Congregation Story

Pastor Terry was pastoring a church with roots as far back as the late 1890s. Over the years, the church had occupied three different locations and had been at its current location for more than fifty years. At one time the church attendance had averaged around 250 in a community of 15,000. The church had left its original denomination over a growing discomfort with some of the theological positions of the denomination. In its heyday this church was known for having the elite of the city's society as its members. The history of this church was one of strife and division that had resulted from power struggles among the members of the congregation and moral failures in the leadership.

Pastor Terry was now faced with a congregation that had declined to approximately fifty people who, for the most part, were content that the church was that size and not growing. They seemed to prefer no-growth to growth that would require some kind of change. It was about this time that Pastor Terry became connected with a group of pastors in a coaching group who were pursuing higher levels of health in their own churches. This coaching group became a lifeline for Terry as he struggled with trying to cast a vision for, and lead, a group of people who didn't seem to want to go anywhere. The congregation was very focused on how the pastor could best serve those who were already a part of the congregation. The coaching group began to be a place of encouragement for Terry, who began to believe that maybe this church could be transformed into a group who could be a significant impact for the kingdom of God in their community.

As a part of the process of the coaching group, a consultation team was sent in to evaluate the church and its ministry. As the consultation weekend progressed, the team found that the vision that Terry had been casting for the people was indeed a God-given vision, and they found themselves reinforcing the information that Terry had already presented to the people and the church leadership. The primary recommendation from the consultation report was for the church to adopt an outwardly focused vision. This was Terry's heart and was the vision God had given him for the future of the church. This recommendation was well received by the leaders and the members of the congregation, and they immediately began to implement the vision that Terry had been casting for some time.

As a result of the new outward focus of the church, new disciples are being made for the kingdom of God. Decisions for Jesus Christ are now occurring at a rate that is about four times higher than before. Attendance has more than doubled and the trend is increasing. The church now has a good relationship with the principal of the local elementary school and is actively helping the school accomplish its purpose in educating and caring for the students of the school. They have a goal of having the same kind of relationship with every school in their city. The church has instituted a prayer program in which letters are sent to people in leadership positions in the city every month. These letters express the church's gratitude for the service each person is providing and a promise to pray for these leaders every day that month. The letters go not just to the high-level leaders but also to those occupying lower positions, who are often forgotten in their efforts. Response to these letters has been very encouraging. Terry's leadership in implementing the recommendations of the consultation and his willingness to implement changes in his own leadership have paid great dividends in the church, the community, and the kingdom of God.

Conclusion
By Paul D. Borden

I hope you have found the stories both beneficial and encouraging as you have read what God is doing to transform congregations and judicatories in what were declining and dying environments. I get to hear these kinds of stories every day. And as a result I am becoming more optimistic about what our God might be doing to revive his church in our lands.

I believe we have a narrow window of opportunity to see God redeem, if that is part of his plan, many of the older established congregations that make up our denominations. The reason I believe the window is a small one is that too many congregations are getting to the point where the cure will kill the patient. Also, as denominations lose more and more dollars, they do not have the resources to implement a health strategy, regardless of whether it works or not.

Denominations must make some key decisions. First, they must stop promoting the program of the year, whether it is good or bad. Denominations, and the congregations that comprise denominations, did not start dying last year and they will not be turned around in a year or two. They need a strategy that will work long-term.

Second, denominations need to make sure that whomever or whatever they employ to bring change is used in an accountable way. If change is not evident (with that change being defined ahead of time), something else should be tried immediately. There is no time to waste, and further delay compounds the need.

Third, those proposing and leading change need the credentials of having done it (in practice, not theory). I am amazed at the number of books I see discussing congregational transformation and pastoral leadership that were written by people that never got a church past the two-hundred barrier. This is also true with consultants and "congregational institutes." We need to require evidence that those posing as experts truly are, based on the fact that they are doing it or have done it.

Fourth, denominations are really going to have to become serious about realizing that change will not come without being willing to both create and support suffering. The passive-aggressive behaviors of most denominations and congregations, which lead to death, are tolerated because no one wants to confront. Also, if denominations and congregations are not willing to lose some of the people they now have, they will never change, never grow, and never reach the thousands of people they are already losing. They are losing them because they are not open to forcing stakeholders to lose their stakes in an enterprise that belongs to Jesus Christ, not them, anyway.

Finally, we must understand that transformation is not enough. It is ultimately about reproduction. Reproduction is the ultimate purpose of focusing on transformation. The church of Jesus Christ will not be revived in our time without a multitude of new congregations being started. That is fundamental. However, we have found it sure is easier to birth healthy, larger babies when the parents themselves are larger and healthier. Transformation can be a foundational key in unlocking a growing movement in congregational reproduction.

"Assaulting the Gates" occurs as healthy pastors and families, lay leaders, denominational leaders, congregations, coaches, mentors, and consultants all work together to form a strategy for transformation and then reproduction. The battle for the souls of people is raging, whether we are engaged in it or not. The zest in congregational life comes as we not only engage, but win. "Assaulting the Gates" allows us to follow the current rules of engagement, because these rules embrace God's mission for the church and they create successful results.

---

[1] Director of Church Transformation, Mid-South District, LCMS; National Director of Revitalization, LCMS.
[2] Director: Growing Healthy Corps Network.
[3] State Pastor of Florida Church of God Ministries.
[4] Senior Pastor of Trinity Fellowship Church, President of TFAC.
[5] Pastor of TFAC Church Health, Secretary of TFAC.
[6] Trinity Fellowship Association of Churches (TFAC)
    5000 Hollywood Rd.
    Amarillo, TX 79118
    (806) 355-8955

APPENDIX A
My Perspective on Congregational Consulting

This appendix contains a set of notes I use at the beginning of our formal training for church consultants. I provide an overview of my understanding of that which is required for consultants. I then provide an overview of the process, focusing on the weekend line-in-the-sand event. This is followed by key assumptions and axioms that relate to the entire process of consulting with congregations.

Introduction

1. The ultimate purpose for consulting is to help a congregation more effectively join God in his mission for the church. This statement assumes:

- I know God's mission for the church.
- I know how to help a congregation join God in this mission.

2. Congregations that are joining God in his mission and are on the upside of their current life cycle need consulting help to become more effective and efficient in how they are accomplishing their mission. My role is to help them get to the next level of effectiveness.

3. Congregations that are either not pursuing God's mission (even though they may be growing and on the upside of their current life cycle) or are on the downside of their current life cycle need consulting help that is best described as an intervention. My role is to help the leaders convert the congregation from one purpose to another (missional change). This involves changing the corporate culture, which is the most difficult kind of change one can lead.

4. Leading congregational change in any form is ultimately a spiritual battle. True success as a consultant is in proportion to the role God the Spirit plays in energizing his church to change. Establishing vehicles to invoke God's help is part of the consulting process. However, once that is done, our focus as consultants must be on developing our skills in order to be the instruments through

whom God works. In most cases God requires both his work and our efforts to produce something lasting.

5. Most pastors cannot lead effective interventions of the congregations they are called to pastor. They need our help for both the short and the long term. However, most congregations will only change in proportion to the leadership ability of the pastor. Leaders (10 percent of all pastors) do not need us, but we can help such leaders speed up the process of change. The rest of the pastors *do* need us, since it often takes a minimum of two people (the pastor and the consultant) to help produce the change.

6. The difference between an effective pastor and an effective consultant is that most effective pastors know how to do ministry well one way, while consultants have seen it done well twenty or more ways. The best consultants are those who have both done it well and understand why it went well and can communicate both the "how" and the "why."

7. Like most things, consulting is an art and a science. The science can be learned; the art is related to how well each consultant implements the science.

The Process

1. The congregation prepares and completes the preassignments given by the consultant a minimum of three weeks before the consultation weekend starts.

- These assignments may include a self-study, surveys, and so forth.
- The consultant must have all the data two weeks before the weekend begins.

2. I read and study the data thoroughly before beginning the consultation. I usually go through it a minimum of three times. In some cases I may seek more information by contacting the pastor or others before I arrive. I then generate:

- A list of 35-70 questions that I want answers to upon my arrival for the weekend
- A preliminary list of strengths and concerns
- Tentative prescriptions

3. Friday is spent interviewing the pastor and other leaders. The number of interviews is related to the size of the congregation. I usually go to dinner with the pastor and the pastor's spouse on Friday evening in order to interview them as a couple. Friday night I conduct at least one focus group. The focus group is made up of twenty to thirty people who represent a cross-section of the congregation. I ask that chairs be arranged in one large horseshoe for people to sit in for the focus group. The only people I do not want in the focus group are leaders I will be interacting with the rest of the weekend. There are three questions I always ask the focus group:

- What is the best thing about your congregation?
- What about your congregation would you change?
- What do you want to see happen in the future with your congregation?

If newer people are present, I also ask them how easy it was for them to become connected to the congregation.

4. I spend Saturday from 9 a.m. to 3 p.m. with the leaders of the congregation. This group should include the pastor, the board, staff members (lay or paid), and other key influencers in the congregation. This is primarily a training day, although I do interview this group initially if I have not had contact with them on Friday. One question I usually add to the others asked in the focus group is about their expectations for the consultation. In the training I want to lay the theological and philosophical groundwork for why their congregation should be healthy, including what health means and looks like. I then spend time providing some analysis of where they are as a congregation and what they need to do to become healthy in order to grow and reproduce. I highly recommend that this session be recorded for those not there and for those who want to go back over what was said after the weekend of consultation is over. I usually want this group sitting at tables arranged in one large horseshoe or square. Lunch should be brought in so time is not wasted in travel to go and eat.

5. Saturday afternoon and evening is spent working on the report. The report usually consists of five strengths, five concerns, and five prescriptions with deadlines for implementation. The report is about two to four pages in length. This report is e-mailed to the pastor

when completed so the pastor has time to interact intellectually and emotionally with the material. I want several of the prescriptions to cause the congregation to be stretched in their behaviors if the report is adopted. I also include a date for the adoption of the report.

6. I do want to preach on Sunday morning. The purpose of the sermon is to generate urgency, cast vision, and prepare the congregation for the report. I want the congregation to be excited about risking for God when I am done preaching. I also meet with the pastor to go over the report that was e-mailed to the pastor on Saturday night. The purpose is to make any cosmetic changes that might help the pastor lead the changes.

After the morning service I want to spend about one and one-half hours with the congregation going over the report. I spend a lot of time attempting to persuade them to adopt the report. I also take time for questions and answers. Everyone receives a written copy of the report.

7. After the report is presented, the first part of the consultation is over. The next phase comes after the congregation adopts the report. A consultant and the judicatory then commit to walk alongside the congregation for a minimum of one year to help them implement the prescriptions. This means that someone needs to be on the campus of the congregation at least once every month for twelve months. The purpose of these visits is to conduct training and to, when necessary, confront leaders who are adopting old habits of behavior. These visits also hold the pastor and other leaders accountable to implement the required changes.

8. The weekend part of the consultation, if done well, creates a large sense of momentum. If that momentum is not replenished with action, and hopefully early victories, however, in the next few months it is lost and almost impossible to regain.

Assumptions

1. Congregations that are not growing are spiritually unhealthy.

2. Congregations that are not growing by consistently and regu-

larly making new disciples for Jesus Christ are disobedient to the Great Commission. The major implication of this assumption is that worship, preaching and teaching the Bible, and fellowship are subordinate to the work of evangelism.

3. Most congregations need to be introduced to the concepts of intentionality and accountability. All accountability starts with a vision that somehow involves a number so that it can be measured.

4. All systemic transformation starts with being clear about the mission or purpose of the congregation. All congregations have the same mission, which is to make new disciples for Jesus Christ. Vision is how the community in which the congregation exists will be changed if the mission is implemented effectively. In my opinion, a number needs to be attached in some way to that vision.

5. An effective consultation is directly related to the consultant's ability to consult well and the pastor(s) ability to lead once the initial weekend is completed. In working with congregations, I am more interested in the ability of the pastor to exercise leadership behavior than I am in the health or lack of such in the congregation.

6. Conducting consultations in free-church traditions is easier, since you do not have to deal with denominational layers that impact the congregation's ability to implement the prescriptions that are suggested.

7. Smaller congregations must be taught to act like the larger congregations they want to become. The basic difference is not one of degrees, breaking certain barriers, but acting large while still small. It is true that the various sociological barriers must be realized. However, the bottom line is either acting like a larger entity or acting like a smaller one.

8. More change is produced with hope than with condemnation. Honesty is crucial, and congregations and leaders must own their sinful or foolish behaviors. However, the motivation for change comes more from the hope for a better tomorrow than from the leaving of a painful past.

9. The best way to get at values, which often seems almost impossible to achieve, is to deal with structure. When structure is changed,

it deals with who is in control (power), who is in charge of resources (money), and who oversees the grounds and facilities (turf).

10. Each consultant must know himself or herself. I must know what I know and what I do not know. I must know how I process and lead others to process the material I am dealing with in the consultation. I must know how I best communicate. I must know what areas of consultation I am good at and when I need to stop consulting and become a broker and networker.

Axioms

1. You can never have enough information. At some point you have to work with what you have, but until you reach that point, you work at obtaining as much data as possible. You also must recognize that not all the data is of equal value. Therefore, you are constantly prioritizing what you know, which often involves making judgments about the person(s) who provided the information.

2. All good consultants listen. This means asking questions and listening to what is said and what is not said. You are also listening and looking for feelings, values, priorities, hurts, and so on.

3. There are certain basic steps to health. How those steps are taken in each consultation varies, however, since each congregation is different. Every consultation is an inductive process and no reports are ever written ahead of time.

4. The consultant must learn when confidentiality is required and when it is a hindrance to the consulting process.

5. It is crucial to know who in the congregation or leadership was the prime motivator for the consultation. I always start the consultation and end most consultations being there to support the pastor. Negative issues with the pastor must be communicated in private and with confidentiality unless the pastor acts without integ-rity. I must also be careful what I tell other congregations and people about previous consultations.

Maxims for the Church Consultant
By Dr. William Hoyt[1]

DNA Defined

What Is DNA?

- Human DNA
  - Every human consists of billions of cells.
  - Each **cell** contains a **nucleus**, inside of which is your own unique set of 46 **chromosomes**.
  - Each chromosome holds an incredibly long molecule of **DNA**, shaped like a compact coil. Sections of the DNA containing complete messages are called **genes.**
  - Human beings have about 9 million kilometers of DNA, enough to go the moon and back 13 times!
  - Your DNA stores all the coded information that determines how you look and how you act.
  - What is with you in the beginning will be with you to the end.
- Churches have DNA
  - Names and faces change, but attitudes and behavior remain the same.

Implications for the Church Consultant

- What is in the beginning will be with you to the end.
  - The more we accurately understand the founding and early history of the church, the better equipped we are to be a transformational influence with them.
    - Church split as the founding principle
      - Authority issues
      - Split again
    - Critical spirit

- • Chew up and spit out leaders, including pastors
  - • Sin in the camp
    - • Same sin over and over
- • What was in the beginning can be strengthened and recaptured.
  - • Timelines
  - • "Oh, that was good! When did we lose that?"
- • DNA does not change without intervention.
  - • Don't mess with health.
  - • Don't expect sin and dysfunction to "just go away."
- • Successful intervention requires a professional.
  - • There is no such thing as self-administered genetic engineering.
  - • We are needed more than they know.
  - • We must keep growing in order to be as prepared as possible to help them.
    - • No one wants a doctor who stopped studying and learning in 1989!

Beliefs Shape

The Way Beliefs Mold

- • Our beliefs shape our reality.
  - • Our beliefs create our mental models of "our reality."
- • We create our own private and very personal world from the beliefs we have of ourselves, our world, and our understanding of "truth."
- • Our beliefs are the often unconscious foundation for our interpretation of "reality," our decisions, and our actions.
- • Our beliefs shape our values and our values drive our actions.
- • What's visible to others grows out of what's invisible in us.
- • What we believe may or may not be true.
- • The more true our beliefs, the more real "our reality."
- • The more we base our beliefs on eternal truths, the healthier and more effective we will be.
- • Our beliefs can free us or limit us.

Limiting	Freeing
I am a wretch and do not deserve to be loved.	I am created by God, who loves me unconditionally.
If it hasn't happened yet, it never will.	Our endlessly creative God still does miracles.
If you knew what I'm really like, you wouldn't accept me.	There are grace-givers out there and I can be transparent around them.
I haven't earned the right to be happy and successful.	God has good plans for me, intervenes in my behalf, and makes the "lines fall for me in pleasant places."
Failure is a really, really, really bad thing.	Failure is nothing more than an opportunity to learn, and all great achievement is born out of risk-taking and willingness to fail.
Better stop hoping; if you get your hopes up, you'll get hurt.	Because God keeps the promises he makes, we can have faith, which is being sure of what we hope for, and certain of what we do not see.
This world, its people, and culture are hopelessly evil, and our goal is to escape it and get to heaven.	God is at work in our world, redeeming people and culture to himself, and he gives us the privilege of being his ambassadors and change agents in this redemptive work.

Implications for Consultants

- Churches have beliefs that shape them; therefore, time spent shaping their beliefs is time well spent.
- Anything of lasting value flows from or can be traced back to an eternal truth.

- Time spent bringing them back to their biblical and theological roots is time well spent.
- Their behavior reveals their actual beliefs.
- Behavior incompatible with their stated beliefs can be used to help them return to their biblical and theological roots.
- A church's beliefs can free them or limit them.

Limiting Beliefs	Freeing Beliefs
We are too small to be involved in church planting.	God expects us to reproduce Christ-followers, leaders, and churches from "Day One"— *ergo*, "birth before buildings."
We don't have any rich people in our church, so we can't afford to do that.	Wealth is in the hands of God, not rich people, and what God wants done, He is fully capable of funding.
If we were in a better location, we would be more effective in reaching the unbelieving and the unchurched.	Effective outreach and evangelism is a matter of the heart and the will, not of location.
We have to grow in order to be strong enough to do something like "that."	We grow and get stronger by doing "that."
We are a Methodist (Baptist, Disciples, Presbyterian, Charismatic, Lutheran, etc.) church.	We are first and foremost a "kingdom" church.

- Bring them back to their core biblical beliefs.

Values Guide

The Value of Values

- You do what you value and you value what you do.
  - No matter what we say we value, what we do betrays our real values.

- Values are the laser beam from which our behavior does not stray.
  - Values are the normative standards that influence the choices people make between perceived alternative courses of action.
  - These "normative standards" may be highly personal or clearly collective.
  - Perceived courses of action may be highly personal or clearly collective.
- Values can be material.
  - Buildings, objects, possessions, assets, etc.
- Values can be abstract.
  - Freedom, peace, love, justice, fairness, equality, etc.

Implications for the Church Consultant

- Individuals and churches choose to do what they do, based on their values.
- The more clear and accurate our understanding of a person or church's values, the more effective we will be as a force for transformational change in their lives.
- For Christians and for churches, our core values should flow out of our core beliefs.
- Often good things cited by churches as "core values" are not core values; they are, at best, "operational values."

Do Such Things As:
- Excellence
- Innovation
- Authenticity
- Tradition
- Integrity

Rise to the Level of Such Things As:
- Loving all people
- Sharing Jesus
- Celebrating joyfully
- Praying faithfully
- Biblical teaching and learning

- Transformed lives
- Being missional servants

Mission Focuses

- The Motivational Power of Mission
- Humans need a sense of purpose.
- We long for meaning in life.
- Sustained effort requires meaning.
- We will go to great lengths when we have an adequate reason to do so.
- Mission defines and imparts purpose and meaning.
- Mission answers "why am I here?" "what is my purpose in life?" "what gives meaning to my life?"
- A compelling sense of mission produces energy.
- A compelling sense of mission produces staying power in troubled or difficult times.

The Dynamic Power of Mission

- A compelling sense of mission focuses life.

Implications for the Church Consultant

- A leader or a church that cannot articulate a concise, clear, and compelling mission will lack direction, energy, and effectiveness.
- Leaders lead more effectively when they can articulate a personal mission statement.
- The unique nuances of a given church's mission will flow out of the personal mission statements of its leaders.
- The personal mission statements of a church's leadership community provide a context for articulating a church's unique vision.
- Time spent helping leaders and churches articulate a biblically based mission is time well spent.

Vision Inspires

The Real Value of Vision

- Vision is a "practical" expression of mission, making the mission more understandable and personal.
- Vision brings the direction of mission into clearer, more specific focus.
- A clear, concise, and compelling vision unites.
- A clear, concise, and compelling vision becomes a leader's "certain trumpet call."
- A clear, concise, and compelling vision ignites passion.
- A clear, concise, and compelling vision increases the likilihood of risk-taking.
- A clear, concise, and compelling vision motivates the giving of self and money.

Implications for the Church Consultant

- If you want to be a transformational influence in the life of the church, you will do whatever it takes to help them articulate a clear, concise, and compelling statement of their vision.
  - IF the vision statement is measurable or can readily be translated into measurable terms
- Few things you leave them will be as valuable to them as a well-constructed, God-inspired vision statement.
  - IF the vision statement is measurable or can readily be translated into measurable terms
- All planning efforts must flow out of their mission and vision, with every activity called for in the plan advancing, in some way, the achieving of their mission and vision.
- Teach them to ask the four fundamental focusing questions:
  - What makes us think that doing this will help us accomplish our mission and vision?
  - Where is the evidence that having done that helped us accomplish our mission and vision?

- What makes us think that spending this money in this way will help us accomplish our mission and vision?
- Where's the evidence that having spent that money in that way helped us accomplish our mission and vision?

Culture Rules

Culture and Its Power

- Culture consists of "the customary beliefs, social forms, and material traits of a racial, religious, or social group." Culture is a group's shared attitudes, values, goals, and practices.
- The power of culture is in direct proportion to the degree to which it is shared.
- Culture defines by excluding those who do not share the culture.
- Every group has a culture that grows in its breadth, depth, and power over time.
  - The older the group, the more powerful the culture.
- Culture change requires the participation of key influencers. Together they can create a critical mass within the group that embraces the new.

Implications for the Church Consultant

- Effectiveness in assessing and guiding transformational change demands a profound understanding of the church's culture.
- Effectiveness in assessing and guiding transformational change demands a profound understanding of the culture of the communities the church seeks to impact.
- The process of "enculturating" the consultant can help the church grow in its understanding of its own culture.
- Cultural understanding is attained by learning the church's history, observation, and asking good questions.

Community Authenticates

The Litmus Test of Community

- The biblical definition of "church" is community.[1]
  - *Ecclesia,* the Greek term from the New Testament translated in English as "church," (as well as the Hebrew term *qahal* from which it derives), means an assembly. There is no clear biblical instance of the term used for a place of meeting or of worship, although in post-apostolic times it early received this meaning.
  - We find the word ecclesia used in the following senses in the New Testament:
    - It is translated "assembly" in the ordinary classical sense (Acts 19:32, 39, 41).
    - It denotes the whole body of the redeemed, all those whom the Father has given to Christ, the invisible catholic church (Eph. 5:23, 25, 27, 29; Heb. 12:23).
    - A few Christians associated together in observing the ordinances of the gospel are an ecclesia (Rom. 16:5; Col. 4:15).
    - All the Christians in a particular city, whether they assembled together in one place or in several places for religious worship, were an ecclesia. Thus all the disciples in Antioch, forming several congregations, were one church (Acts 13:1); so also we read of the "church of God that is in Corinth" (1 Cor. 1:2), "the church in Jerusalem" (Acts 8:1), "the church in Ephesus" (Rev. 2:1), etc.
    - The whole body of professing Christians throughout the world (1 Cor. 15:9; Gal. 1:13; Matt. 16:18) are the church of Christ.
- A church that is not a community (does not practice community) has the form of a church but lacks the substance of a church.
- The most effective hermeneutic of the gospel is a community that seeks to live by it.
- The growing postmodern culture values community and ascribes value and authenticity when it perceives it to be present.

- Postmoderns are not necessarily experts in community, especially true biblical community, but they are clearly in search of it.

Implication for Church Consultants

- Most of us have little history in dealing with the issue of community in churches. We have a huge learning curve ahead of us.
- Future effectiveness will require our addressing the issue of community in the life of the churches with which we work.

Systems Sustain

The Staying Power of Systems

- A system is an established, repetitive way of doing something.
- A system is an interactive, interdependent set of actions, procedures, and policies that form a unified whole.
- A system consists of the things we typically do in order to accomplish a specific desired outcome.
- Systems create equilibrium.
- Systems allow us to go on "auto-pilot" on the repetitive things so we can focus on the big-picture things.
- All churches have systems, either intentionally or by default.
- Default systems are almost always dysfunctional and debilitating.
- Intentionally designed systems, if utilized, sustain effectiveness over time and through leadership changes.

Implications for the Church Consultant

- Helping a church establish the basic nine systems will prove one of the most transformational things you can do.
  - Evangelism
  - Worship
  - Assimilation
  - Lay Mobilization

- Spiritual Formation (Disciple-making)
- Leader Development
- Congregational Care
- Communication
- Decision-making

---

1. NexStep Coaching and Consulting; www.nexstepcoaching.org

A Sample Covenant for Pastors in a Cluster

TFAC Church Health Initiative

"A plan to win the region for Christ through missional churches and leaders."

VISION: For TFAC and its members to partner together in winning this region for Christ through relationships, prayer, and the equipping of pastors and leaders to grow healthy, reproductive churches.

Covenant Commitment by TFAC Pastors

- Pastors agree to attend all monthly coaching group meetings.
- Pastors agree to fulfill all reading and ministry assignments.
- Pastors agree to pray for their Coaching Group partner each week.
- Pastors will pray publicly for one Coaching Group congregation each week.
- Pastors agree to report basic statistics to the TFAC office each week.
- Pastors agree to submit to the Church Consultation process.
- Pastors agree to encourage their congregations to attend Lay Training events.
- Pastors agree to honor their church's financial commitment to TFAC.

Covenant Commitment by TFAC

- To financially and structurally support the Coaching Group meetings, which includes:
  - Cover all coaching pastor and consultant fees and expenses
  - Provide books for required reading
  - Provide handouts, outlines, and other teaching materials

- Furnish all meals
- Financially support two large lay-training events, which include:
  - Speaker's fees and expenses
  - Outlines and other teaching materials
  - DVD and CD recordings of the events
- Partner with coaching groups and churches in selecting locations and personnel for planting new churches in the region.

_____   _____

Name of Church   Date

_____   _____

Senior Pastor   Executive Pastor of TFAC